MOON

OUTDOORS

TAKE A HIKE
SEATTLE

SCOTT LEONARD

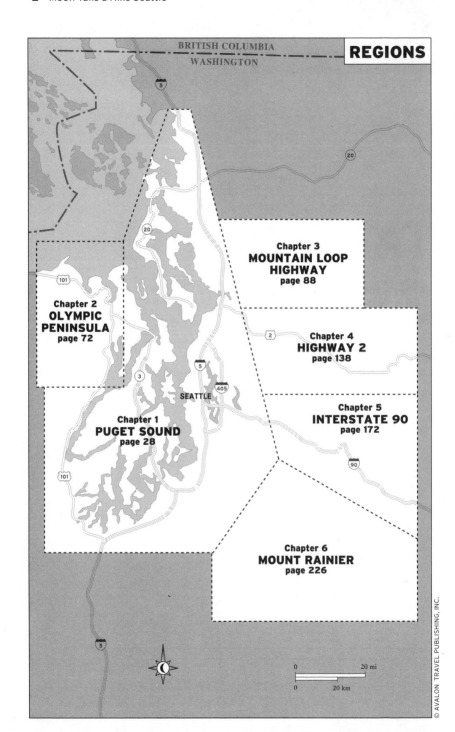

REGIONS

BRITISH COLUMBIA
WASHINGTON

Chapter 3
MOUNTAIN LOOP HIGHWAY
page 88

Chapter 2
OLYMPIC PENINSULA
page 72

Chapter 4
HIGHWAY 2
page 138

SEATTLE

Chapter 5
INTERSTATE 90
page 172

Chapter 1
PUGET SOUND
page 28

Chapter 6
MOUNT RAINIER
page 226

0   20 mi

0   20 km

© AVALON TRAVEL PUBLISHING, INC.

Contents

How to Use This Book

ABOUT THE MAPS

This book is divided into chapters based on regions that are within close reach of the city; an overview map of these regions precedes the table of contents. Each chapter begins with a region map that shows the locations and numbers of the trails listed in that chapter.

Each trail profile is also accompanied by a detailed trail map that shows the hike route.

For a directory of map symbols, please see page 249.

ABOUT THE TRAIL PROFILES

Each profile includes a narrative description of the trail's setting and terrain. This description also typically includes mile-by-mile hiking directions, as well as information about the trail's highlights and unique attributes.

The trails marked by the **BEST ◖** symbol are highlighted in the author's Best Hikes list.

Options

If alternative routes are available, this section is used to provide information on side trips or note how to shorten or lengthen the hike.

Directions

This section provides detailed driving directions to the trailhead from the city center or from the intersection of major highways. When public transportation is available, instructions will be noted here.

Information and Contact

This section provides information on fees, facilities, and access restrictions for the trail. It also includes the name of the land management agency or organization that oversees the trail, as well as an address, phone number, and website if available.

ABOUT THE ICONS
The icons in this book are designed to provide at-a-glance information on special features for each trail.

⬛ The trail climbs to a high overlook with wide views.

⬛ The trail offers an opportunity for wildlife watching.

⬛ The trail features wildflower displays in spring.

⬛ The trail visits a body of water.

⬛ The trail travels to a waterfall.

⬛ The trail visits a historic site.

⬛ Dogs are allowed.

⬛ The trailhead can be accessed via public transportation.

⬛ The trail is wheelchair-accessible.

⬛ The trail is appropriate for children.

⬛ The trail is open to snowshoers in winter.

ABOUT THE DIFFICULTY RATING
Each profile also includes a difficulty rating. The ratings are defined as follows:

Easy: Easy hikes are four miles or less round-trip, with the exception of a few easy river hikes that are 10 miles round-trip, and have less than 500 feet of elevation gain. They are generally suitable for families with small children and hikers seeking a mellow stroll.

Easy/Moderate: Easy/Moderate hikes are between three and eight miles round-trip and have up to 1,500 feet of elevation gain. They are generally suitable for families with active children above the age of six and hikers who are reasonably fit.

Moderate: Moderate hikes are between 5 and 13 miles round-trip and have 1,500–2,000 feet of elevation gain. They are generally suitable for adults and children who are fit.

Moderate/Strenuous: Strenuous hikes are between 5 and 10 miles round-trip and have 2,000–3,000 feet of elevation gain. They are suitable for very fit hikers who are seeking a workout.

Strenuous: Strenuous hikes are between 7 and 16 miles round-trip and have 3,000 feet or more of elevation gain. These hikes are suitable only for advanced hikers who are very physically fit.

The level of difficulty for any trail can change considerably due to weather or trail conditions. Always phone ahead to check on current trail and weather conditions.

INTRODUCTION

Author's Note

Our Pacific Northwest is America's most beautiful region. Now, I admit that I may harbor a little bias as a Northwest native. But where else can one find a mix of saltwater and mountains so closely at hand? Where else are there so many opportunities to get out near a large city? Our metropolis is a special one, and many Washingtonians love nothing more than spending time in it. Whether you hike once a year or once a week, there are many great places to explore and *Moon Take a Hike Seattle* can help you access the treasure we have all around us. It's the only guide you'll need to get out on the trail for a day of hiking.

I used only two limitations when selecting hikes for this book: that the hikes can be accomplished in one day and that the trailhead be within two hours of Seattle. There are many different lengths of hikes here—some can be fit into a quick morning outing while others are full-day adventures. All trailheads are easy to access. The only exceptions to the two-hour rule were hikes I included from the Olympic Peninsula. The ferry ride to Kingston adds extra time to the trip, but the Peninsula is such a great place I felt they had to be included.

This guide is not meant to be an exhaustive list of every hike near our city. Instead, I've selected a diverse set of hikes that includes only the best and most exciting hikes in our region. I'm confident that you'll enjoy every one. There are easy hikes for beginners and families and difficult and strenuous hikes for hard-core enthusiasts. Some hikes stroll along rivers or the Puget Sound while others ramble up to the Cascades' most beautiful meadows and peaks.

For each hike, you'll find all the information you need to hit the trail. I've included clear directions to the trailhead, any fees or regulations you need to know about, and a detailed description of the hike. Each listing has its own map to help you find your way on the trail. All of this information is organized in a way that is easy for you to find quickly.

Writing this book was a kick for me because I love sharing hikes and adventures with others. I hope that *Moon Take a Hike Seattle* winds up dog-eared and living in your backseat, always leading you to a new adventure in our beautiful outdoors.

Best Hikes

◖ Best Easy Hikes
Lighthouse Point, Puget Sound chapter, page 37.
Squak Mountain, Puget Sound chapter, page 53.
Brown Farm Dike Trail, Puget Sound chapter, page 66.
Twin Falls, Interstate 90 chapter, page 176.
Green Lake Trail, Mount Rainier chapter, page 230.

◖ Best Hikes for Berry Picking
Mount Forgotten Meadows, Mountain Loop Highway chapter, page 121.
Mount Dickerman, Mountain Loop Highway chapter, page 124.
West Cady Ridge, Highway 2 chapter, page 151.
Pratt Lake, Interstate 90 chapter, page 198.
Commonwealth Basin, Interstate 90 chapter, page 208.

◖ Best Hikes to Lakes
Lake 22, Mountain Loop Highway chapter, page 111.
Foss Lakes, Highway 2 chapter, page 160.
Annette Lake, Interstate 90 chapter, page 200.
Denny Creek Trail to Melakwa Lake, Interstate 90 chapter, page 202.
Snow Lake, Interstate 90 chapter, page 205.

◖ Best Hikes for Viewing Wildflowers
Mount Townsend, Olympic Peninsula chapter, page 78.
Goat Flats, Mountain Loop Highway chapter, page 104.
Tolmie Peak, Mount Rainier chapter, page 235.
Spray Park, Mount Rainier chapter, page 237.
Noble Knob, Mount Rainier chapter, page 243.

◖ Best Hikes to Waterfalls
Boulder River, Mountain Loop Highway chapter, page 92.
Woody Trail to Wallace Falls, Highway 2 chapter, page 145.
Lake Serene Trail, Highway 2 chapter, page 147.

Twin Falls, Interstate 90 chapter, page 176.

Denny Creek Trail to Melakwa Lake, Interstate 90 chapter, page 202.

◖ Best Kid-Friendly Hikes

Bluff Loop, Puget Sound chapter, page 42.

Big Tree Loop, Puget Sound chapter, page 56.

Dungeness Spit, Olympic Peninsula chapter, page 74.

Talapus Lake, Interstate 90 chapter, page 194.

Greenwater Trail, Mount Rainier chapter, page 241.

◖ Best Strenuous Hikes

Stujack Pass, Mountain Loop Highway chapter, page 98.

Mount Dickerman, Mountain Loop Highway chapter, page 124.

Gothic Basin, Mountain Loop Highway chapter, page 126.

Blanca Lake, Highway 2 chapter, page 149.

Granite Mountain, Interstate 90 chapter, page 196.

Hiking Tips

THE 10 ESSENTIALS

The 10 Essentials are just that—indispensable items that you should carry every time you hit the trail. No matter where you're headed, you never know what you're going to come across (or what's going to come across you); being prepared can help to prevent problems before they start.

Proper Clothing

Here in Washington, the weather can turn at the drop of a hat. In every season, rain seems never more than a few hours away. We didn't get a reputation for wet weather for nothing. During the summer, thundershowers or snowstorms can give even experienced hikers a surprise. So it's best to bring extra clothing for those unexpected weather fronts.

Clothing that can ward off the cold is extremely important. Most accidents in the wilderness are the result of, or complicated by, hypothermia, which can set in quickly and with little warning. Once a person starts getting cold, the ability to think and troubleshoot heads downhill. Symptoms of hypothermia include fatigue, drowsiness, unwillingness to go on, a feeling of deep cold or numbness, poor coordination, and mumbling. To avoid this, bring clothes that are easily layered. During the summer, that can be as simple as a warm fleece. During the winter, wool or synthetic fleeces are effective against the cold. A stocking cap is extremely helpful since a big chunk of body heat is lost through the head. Extra socks are helpful for keeping feet warm and comfortable. Remember that you can be vulnerable even in the summer—bitter July snowstorms are not unheard-of.

Rain gear, such as a jacket, pants, and a hat or hood, is equally important during all seasons, but especially during the fall and spring when it's practically impossible to head outdoors without rain. Even if there is no rain in the forecast, be prepared for it. (Local weather reporters are forecasting for the cities, not the mountains.) And short but serious rainstorms in any season are the norm, not the exception, in Washington.

When dressing for a hike, it's important to avoid cotton clothing, especially if rain is a possibility. Once cotton gets wet, it can draw off body heat, causing hypothermia to set in quickly. Wool and polypropylene are good alternatives. If you get wet wearing cotton, take it off if you have another layer that is not cotton.

Water Supply

Be sure to drink lots of water, even if it's not that hot out. Staying properly hydrated can prevent heat exhaustion. Symptoms of heat exhaustion include

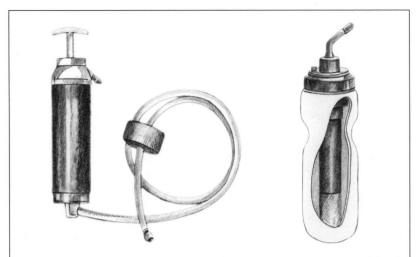

Water filters are a wise investment since all wilderness water should be considered contaminated. Make sure the filter can be easily cleaned or has a replaceable cartridge. The filter pores must be 0.4 microns or less to remove bacteria.

excessive sweating, gradual weakness, nausea, anxiety, and eventually loss of consciousness. Usually, the skin becomes pale and clammy or cold, the pulse slows, and blood pressure may drop. Heat exhaustion is often unexpected but very serious; someone experiencing heat exhaustion will have difficulty getting out of a wilderness setting and will need assistance—not always an easy task.

When day hiking, you can probably carry from the trailhead all the water you'll need for the hike. Two to three liters per person is a good rule of thumb. Carrying water with you or having a method of filtering water is important— never drink untreated water in the wild. A stream may look crystal clear and be ice cold, but it can also be full of nasty parasites and viruses. If you catch a good case of *giardia* or *cryptosporidia,* you could be incapacitated for a full week. Carrying a stove or a filter can be impractical on day hikes. The best back-up method is to carry iodine and chlorine that quickly and easily purify water. They're lightweight and come in handy in a pinch. If you don't mind a strange taste in your water, these will do the trick.

Extra Food

The lore of the backcountry is filled with tales of folks who head out for a quick day hike and end up spending a night (or more) in the wilderness. Planning on just an afternoon away from the kitchen, they don't bring enough food to last into the night or morning. Not only is an empty stomach a restless stomach, it can be dangerous, as well. A full stomach provides energy to help ward off hypothermia and keeps the mind clear for the task at hand: Not getting even more lost.

When packing food for an outing, include a little extra gorp or an extra energy bar. This will come in extremely handy on that night you're wandering back to the trailhead later than planned. A grizzled old veteran of the backcountry once passed on a helpful tip when it comes to packing extra food. Extra food is meant for an emergency; the last thing you want to do is eat it in a nonemergency because it looked good and then need it later. So, he packed something nutritious that he'd consider eating only in an emergency: canned dog food.

Fire Starter

Some people prefer matches while others choose to bring along a lighter. Either way, it's important to have something with which to start a fire. Don't think that you can start your fire by rubbing two sticks together. Even when it's dry, sticks don't like to start up easily. So be certain to purchase some quality waterproof matches (you can make your own with paraffin wax and wooden matches), or carry a couple of lighters. Regardless of your choice, keep them packed away in a safe and dry place (like a sandwich baggie). Besides a starter, bring along something to keep the fire going for a bit. Fire pellets are available at any outdoor store. Do-it-yourselfers will be glad to know that toilet paper is highly flammable, as are cotton balls dipped in Vaseline. Starting a fire when it's cold, dark, and wet can save your life.

Map and Compass

You need to carry a map and compass on your person *every* time you hit the trail, whether you're going up Mount Si with the rest of Seattle or venturing into the vacant backcountry of the North Cascades National Park. No matter how familiar you think you are with a trail, you can get lost. Not only should you carry the two, but you also need to know how to use them.

A map is not always a map. You can't rely on the map that AAA gave you out on the trail. Instead, it's best to purchase a quality topographic map for use on the trail. A quality topographic map allows hikers to follow their steps more accurately and is infinitely more helpful for figuring out where you are when you're lost. Green Trails of Seattle makes high-quality topo maps for 90 percent of Washington trails. The USGS and National Geographic also make good topo maps.

Now that it's the 21st century, GPS devices are becoming more popular.

These are great toys to play with while out on the trail. Some folks even swear by them. But a GPS device often won't work in a thick forest canopy. A good old-fashioned compass, on the other hand, is significantly cheaper and won't ever die on you when the batteries run out.

First-Aid Kit

A first-aid kit is an important essential to carry while out on the trail. With twigs, rocks, and bears lurking around every corner, hiking can be dangerous business. Injuries can range from small abrasions to serious breaks, and a simple but well-stocked first-aid kit can be a lifesaver. It's best to purchase a first-aid kit at an outdoors store. Kits come in different sizes, depending on your use, and include the fundamentals. Also, a number of organizations provide medical training for backcountry situations. Courses run from one-day seminars in simple first aid all the way to month-long classes for wilderness EMT certification. Outdoor enthusiasts who go out on a regular basis should consider a course in Wilderness First Aid (WOOFA) or Wilderness First Response (WOOFER).

Band-aids come in every kit but are only helpful for small, nonserious cuts or abrasions. Here are a few things that are especially important and can come in handy in an emergency:

- Ibuprofen: It works very well to combat swelling. Twist an ankle or suffer a nasty bruise and reducing the swelling quickly becomes an important consideration.
- Athletic tape and gauze: These are helpful in treating twisted or strained joints. A firm wrap with athletic tape will make the three-mile hobble to the car less of an ordeal.
- Travel-size supplies of general medicines: Items like Alka-Seltzer or NyQuil are multipurpose and practical.

Finally: the only thing better than having a first-aid kit on the trail is not needing one.

Sun Protection

Most hikers don't think that fierce sunburns are a serious concern in notoriously gray Washington. But during the summer, the sun can be extremely brutal, especially at higher altitudes where a few thousand feet of atmosphere can be sorely missed. A full day in the blazing sun is hard on the eyes as well.

Don't let the sun spoil an otherwise great day in the outdoors. Sunscreen is worth its weight in gold out on the trail. Be sure to apply it regularly, and keep kids lathered up as well. It helps to bring a hat and lightweight clothing with long sleeves, both of which can make sunscreen almost unnecessary. Finally, many hikers swear by a good pair of sunglasses. Perhaps obvious during the summer, sunglasses are also a snowshoer's best friend. Snow blindness is a serious threat on beautiful sunny days during the winter.

All of these measures will make a trip not only safer but more enjoyable as well. Avoiding sunburn is also extremely helpful in warding off heat stroke, a serious condition in the backcountry.

Light Source

Countless times even veteran hikers intend to go out only for a "quick" day hike and end up finishing in the dark. There were just too many things to see, too many lakes to swim in, and too many peaks to bag on that "short" hike. Often, getting back to the car or camp before it's dark requires the difficult task of leaving a beautiful place while it's still light out. Or perhaps while out on an easy forest hike, you're on schedule to get back before dark, but the thick forest canopy brings on night an hour or two early. There are lots of ways to get stuck in the outdoors in the dark. And what good are a map and compass if you can't see them? Plan ahead and bring an adequate light source. The market is flooded these days with cheap (and not so cheap) headlamps. Headlamps are basically small flashlights that fit around your head. They're great because they're bright and they keep your hands free to beat back brush on the trail or hungry fellow campers around the dinner stove.

Multipurpose Knife

For outdoors enthusiasts, the multipurpose Swiss army knife is one of the greatest ideas since sliced bread. Handy utility knives come in all shapes and sizes and are made by about a hundred different companies. A high-quality utility knife will come in handy in a multitude of situations. The features available include big knives and little knives, saws and scissors, corkscrews and screwdrivers, and about 30 other fun little tools. They are useful almost everywhere, except at the airport.

Emergency Kit

You'll probably have a hard time finding a pre-prepared emergency kit for sale at any store. Instead, this is something that you can quickly and inexpensively assemble yourself.

- Space blanket: Find these at any outdoor store or army surplus store. They're small, shiny blankets that insulate extremely well, are highly visible, and will make do in place of a tent when needed.

- Signal mirror: A signal mirror is handy when you're lost. Catch the glare of the sun, and you can signal your position to search-and-rescue hikers or planes. The small mirror that comes attached to some compasses works perfectly.
- Whistle: Again, if you get really lost, don't waste your breath screaming and hollering. You'll lose your voice quickly, and it doesn't carry far anyhow. Blow your whistle all day or night long, and you'll still be able to talk to the trees (or yourself).

BEARS AND COUGARS

Hiking is all about being outdoors. Fresh air, colorful wildflowers, expansive mountain views, and a little peace and quiet are what folks are after as they embark on the trail. The great outdoors is also home to creatures big and small. Nearly all wildlife around Seattle is completely harmless to hikers; bears and cougars are the only wildlife that pose a danger to us humans. Fortunately, the vast majority of all encounters with these big predators are nothing more than a memorable story. Coming across bears and cougars may be frightening, but these encounters don't need to be dangerous as long as you follow a few simple precautions.

Bears

Running into a bear is the most common worry of novice hikers when they hit the trail. Bears are big, furry, and naturally a bit scary at first sight. But in reality, bears want little to do with people and much prefer to avoid us altogether. The chance of getting into a fistfight with a bear is rare in Washington. In our state's history, there have only been three attacks and one fatality recorded. As long as you stay away from bear cubs and food, bears will almost certainly leave you alone.

What kind of bears will you see out on the trail? Most likely it will be a black bear, but Washington is home to grizzly bears as well. Black bears, whose thick coats range from light tan to cinnamon to black, are by far the most numerous, with approximately 25,000 spread throughout our state. Grizzly bears are much more rare, numbering less than 50, and are primarily located along the Canadian border in the Pasayten Wilderness and Selkirk Mountains. Grizzlies have a distinctive hump on their shoulder.

The old image of Yogi the Bear stealing picnic baskets is not that far off. Bears love to get a hold of human food, so proper food storage is an effective way to avoid an unwanted bear encounter. When camping, be sure to use a bear hang. Collect all food, toiletries, and anything else with scent; place it all in a stuff sack and hang the sack in a tree. The sack should be at least 12 feet off the ground and eight feet from the tree trunk.

BLACK BEAR

Straight Profile

No Hump

3¾ in.

3½ in.

7 in.

Grizzly bears are distinguished from **black bears** by a pronounced shoulder hump and a concave facial profile. Grizzlies are generally brown and average 10 to 11 feet in length, while black bears (which can also be brown) attain lengths of five to seven feet.

Hump

Dish Face Profile

GRIZZLY BEAR

5½ in.

5¼ in.

9¾ in.

Note: Color of bears can't be used for identification.

Should you come across a bear on the trail, stay calm. It's okay to be scared, but with a few precautions, you will be completely safe. First, know that your object is not to intimidate the bear but simply to let it know you are not easy prey. Make yourself look big by standing tall, waving your arms, or even holding open your jacket. Second, don't look it in the eye. Bears consider eye contact to be aggressive and an invitation to a confrontation. Third, speak loudly and firmly to the bear. Bears are nearsighted and can't make out objects from afar. But a human voice means humans, and a bear is likely to retreat from your presence. If a bear advances, it is very likely only trying to get a better look. Finally, if the bear doesn't budge, go around it in a wide circle. In case the unlikely should occur and the bear attacks, curl up in a ball, stay as still as possible, and wait for the attack to end. If the bear bites, take a cheap shot at the nose. Bears hate being hit on their sensitive noses. Trying to hit a bear from this position is difficult. It can work if you can cover your neck with one hand and swing with the other. Protecting yourself is first priority. If the bear is especially aggressive, it's necessary to fight back. Most importantly, don't let fear of bears prevent you from getting out there; it's rare to see a bear and even rarer to have a problem with one.

Cougars

With millions of acres of wilderness, Washington is home to cougars, bobcats, and lynx. Bobcats and lynx are small and highly withdrawn. If you encounter one of these recluses, you're in a small minority. Cougars are also very shy, and encounters with these big cats are rare; only 2,500 cougars live in our state. Cougar attacks are extremely uncommon; there have been few in recent years and only one fatality ever in Washington. You're more likely to be struck by lightning than attacked by a cougar. In most circumstances, you're just going to have a great story.

If you should encounter a cougar in the wild, you want to intimidate it as much as possible. First, don't run! A cougar views something running from it as dinner. Second, get big by waving your arms, jumping around, and spreading open a jacket. Cougars have very little interest in a tough fight. Third, don't bend down to pick up a rock; you'll only look smaller to the cougar. Fourth, stare the cougar down—a menacing stare-down is intimidating for a cougar. Finally, should a cougar attack, fight back with everything you have and as dirtily as possible.

PROTECTING THE OUTDOORS

It's Friday afternoon, work has been a trial all week, and there's only one thing on your mind: getting outdoors and hitting the trail for the weekend. For many of us, nature is a getaway from the confines of urban living. The irony of it all, however, is that the more people head to the backcountry, the less wild it truly is. That means that it takes a collective effort from all trail users to keep the outdoors as pristine as it was 100 years ago. This effort is so important, in fact, that the organization Leave No Trace has created an ideology for low-impact use of our wilderness. (For more information on the Leave No Trace Center for Outdoor Ethics and their values, check out their website at www.lnt.org.) Here are a few principles that we all can follow to ensure that the great outdoors continues to be great.

Planning Your Trip

A little careful planning and preparation not only makes your trip safer, but it also makes it easy to minimize resource damage. Make sure you know the regulations, such as group size limits or campfire regulations, before hitting the trail. Prepare for any special circumstances an area may have, such as the need for ice axes or water filters. Many places are used heavily during summer weekends. Schedule your trip for a weekday or off-season, and you'll encounter far fewer fellow bipeds.

Hiking and Camping

One of the most important principles for hikers and campers here in Washington is to minimize our impact on the land. Many of our greatest and most heavily used trails visit fragile environments, such as alpine meadows and lakeshores. These ecosystems are easily injured by walking or camping. Take care to travel only on the main trail, never cut a switchback, and avoid the social trails—small, unofficial trails that are made over years by hikers cutting trails—that spiderweb through many a high meadow. When camping, pitch camp in already established sites, never on a meadow. Take care in selecting a site for a camp kitchen and when heading off for the bathroom. Being aware of your impact not only improves the experience for yourself but also for those who follow you.

Taking Out Your Trash

It goes without saying that trash does not belong in the great outdoors. That goes for all trash, regardless of whether it's biodegradable or not. From food packaging to the food itself, it has to go out the way it came in: on your back. Ditto for toilet paper. As far as human waste goes, dig a cat hole for your waste, and pack all toilet paper and hygiene products in bags. It may be nasty, but it's only fair for others.

Leaving What You Find

The old saying goes, "Take only photographs and leave only footprints." Well, if you're walking on durable surfaces such as established trails, you won't even leave footprints. And it's best to leave the artifacts of nature where they belong: in nature. By doing so, you ensure that others can enjoy them as well. If you see something interesting, remember that it is only there because the hiker in front of you left it for you to find. The same goes for attractive rocks, deer and elk antlers, and wildflowers. Avoid altering sites by digging trenches, building lean-tos, or harming trees.

Lighting Campfires

Thanks to Smokey the Bear, we all know the seriousness of forest fires. If you're going to have a fire, make sure it's out before going to sleep or leaving camp. But there are other important considerations for campfires. Here in Washington, many national forests and wildernesses have fire bans above 3,500 feet. At these higher altitudes, trees grow slowly and depend greatly on decomposition of downed trees. Burning downed limbs and trees robs the ecosystems of much-needed nutrients, an impact that lasts centuries. Carry a camp stove any time you plan on cooking while backpacking.

Encountering Wildlife

No chasing the deer. No throwing rocks at the chipmunks. No bareback riding the elk. And no wrestling the bears. In all seriousness, the most important way we can respect wildlife is by not feeding them. Chipmunks may be cute, but feeding them only makes them fat and dependent on people for food. Keep a clean camp without food on the ground, and be sure to hang food anytime you're separated from it. A good bear hang is as much about keeping the bears out of the food as it is about keeping the mice and squirrels from eating it.

Respecting Other Hikers

If you are considerate of others on the trail, they are likely to return the favor. This includes such simple things as yielding right-of-way to those who are trudging uphill, keeping noise to a minimum, and observing any use regulations, such as no mountain bikes or no fires. If possible, try to set up camp off trail and out of sight. Together, everyone can equally enjoy the beauties of hiking in Washington.

HIKING WITH DOGS

Though not everyone may have a dog, nearly everyone has an opinion about dogs on the trail. Hiking with canine friends can be a great experience, not only for us but for them, as well. What dog doesn't love being out on the trail, roaming the wild and in touch with his ancestral roots? That's great, but there are a few matters that must be considered before taking a dog out on the trail.

First, be aware that national parks do not allow dogs on any trail at any time. However, dogs are allowed throughout national forests and any wildernesses contained within them. Second, dogs should remain on the trail at all times. Dogs can create an enormous amount of erosion when roaming off trail, and they're frequent switchback cutters. Third, dogs must be under control at all times. Leashes are not always mandatory because many dogs are obedient and do very well while unleashed. But if you're not going to use a leash, your dog should respond to commands well and not bother other hikers. Finally, be aware that dogs and wildlife don't mix well. Dogs love to chase chipmunks, rabbits, deer, and anything else that moves. But from the chipmunk's point of view, a big, slobbering beast chasing you is stressful and unequivocally bad. Not only that, but dogs can incite aggression in bears or cougars. An unleashed dog can quickly transform a peaceful bear into a raging assault of claws and teeth. Plus, bears and cougars find dogs to be especially tasty. Don't hesitate to bring your dog out on the trail as long as you take the dog's interests, as well as other hikers' interests, into consideration.

PERMITS

You've got your pack ready, done your food shopping, purchased the right maps, and even wrestled the kids into the car. But do you have the right permits? Here in Washington, there are several permits that you may need before you can hit the trail. Headed for a national forest? Read up on the Northwest Forest Pass. Driving down to Mount Rainier or the Olympics? You probably need a National Parks Pass. Backpacking in a national park? Don't forget your backcountry camping permit.

Northwest Forest Pass

The Northwest Forest Pass (NWFP) is the most widely used permit in our state. The pass is accepted at 680 day-use recreation sites in Washington and Oregon. Almost every trailhead in every national forest in Washington requires a NWFP for parking. Remarkably, a Northwest Forest Pass is all that is required in the North Cascades National Park. The Colville National Forest is the one agency that is not participating in the NWFP program; access to trailheads in the Colville is free. Senior citizens take note: in lieu of a NWFP, the federal Golden Eagle, Golden Access, and Golden Age passes are accepted.

The Northwest Forest Pass costs $30 and is valid for one year from date of purchase. It's interchangeable between vehicles in the same household. Day passes may also be purchased at a cost of $5 per day. More than 240 vendors across the northwest offer the pass, including all ranger stations, most outdoor stores, and many service stations in recreational areas. Passes can also be ordered online through Nature of the Northwest at www.naturenw.org. Proceeds from Northwest Forest Passes go toward improvements at recreational sites, including refurbishing trailheads, trail maintenance and construction, and environmental education. There is a lot of controversy over the pass, as critics contend that national forests are public lands and already paid for by federal taxes. They have a point, but the revenue serves to supplement ever-dwindling forest service budgets.

National Parks Passes and Permits

No question, the United States has the world's premier national park system. From Acadia National Park in Maine to Denali National Park in Alaska, the United States has taken care to preserve our most important ecosystems for future generations to enjoy. Here in Washington, we have North Cascades, Olympic, and Mount Rainier National Parks to savor. This book includes coverage only of Mount Rainier National Park. The four hikes inside the park require fees for car access to the trailheads. Access to Carbon River Road and Mowich Lake Road require one of three passes: A Single Visit Vehicle Permit ($10 and good for seven days), a Mount Rainier National Park Annual Pass ($30 and good for one year), or any of the national parks passes, which are good for one year at all national parks in the United States. National parks passes include: the National Parks Pass ($50 and good at any national park in the United States for one year), the Golden Access Pass (available for people who are blind or permanently disabled and allows lifetime admittance to any national park for free), and the Golden Age Pass (available to people 62 years or older and allows lifetime admittance to any national park for a one-time fee of $10).

PUGET SOUND

© SCOTT LEONARD

BEST HIKES

Who says you have to go far from Seattle to enjoy

the great outdoors? The Puget Sound area is undoubtedly one of the United States' most scenic locales for a major urban center, which is great for Seattleites. From trails along Puget Sound to quiet forest rambles and even a few mountain peaks in the Issaquah Alps, there are lots of options for quick day trips out on the trail without wandering far from home. Thanks to easy trails and loads of wildlife, these places are excellent trips for young hikers-in-training.

Right in Seattle's backyard are the beloved Issaquah Alps. The peaks run from Lake Washington east to the Cascades and include Cougar Mountain, Squak Mountain, Tiger Mountain, and Rattlesnake Mountain. Referring to these peaks as alps is a play on the mountains' diminutive stature – Tiger and Rattlesnake barely scrape above 3,000 feet of elevation. Still, there are miles and miles of hiking trails throughout the forested mountains. Cougar is remarkably close and easily accessible for a short hike or run. Squak Mountain is lesser-known but has big lush forests and quiet hiking trails, and Tiger Mountain has numerous trails and is a great place for family hiking.

If beach and bay views are a draw, Whidbey Island, one of America's longest islands and the jewel of the Puget Sound, is a short drive away. With miles of shoreline and dramatic settings, the abundance of easy hikes makes this an excellent place for families. It is also an ideal retreat in the rainy season because the Olympic Mountains help shield it from heavy rain. Shoreline trails like Lighthouse Point and Goose Rock at Deception Pass State Park offer windswept trees and opportunities to see wildlife like sea otters and orcas. Farther south on Whidbey Island is Fort Ebey State Park, with the memorable Bluff Trail high above the waters of Puget Sound. And Wilbert Trail at South Whidbey Island State Park wanders through stands of impressive old-growth forest.

Back on the mainland are several great hiking areas and wildlife refuges. Just south of Bellingham is Chuckanut Mountain, a favorite hangout for Bellingham locals, with a pair of nice hikes to beautiful Lost or Fragrance Lakes. The Puget Sound region sees millions of birds pass through the area each spring and fall on their way to warmer climes. Refuges like Padilla Bay near Mount Vernon and Nisqually Wildlife Refuge near Olympia offer exceptional opportunities for quiet walks and wildlife sightings. Ducks and geese might be lounging in the marshlands while goshawks and falcons patrol the air in search of dinner. And let's not forget one of America's finest urban parks, Point Defiance Park in Tacoma. The Outer Perimeter Trail features big trees and great views of the Narrows.

With all that the Puget Sound area has to offer so close to home, there's no excuse to stay indoors.

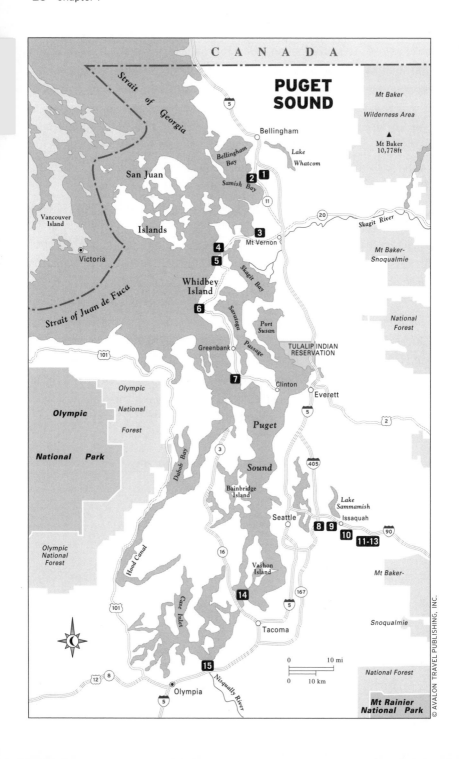

Puget Sound Hikes

1 CEDAR LAKE
Chuckanut Mountain

🏕 🦌 🏂 🐎

Level: Moderate   **Total Distance:** 4.4 miles

Hiking Time: 2.5 hours   **Elevation Gain:** 1,300 feet

Summary: A sharp ascent through leafy forest to quiet Cedar Lake, with an optional climb to views of Puget Sound.

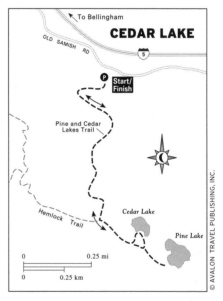

Chuckanut Mountain is best known for its colorful drive along Puget Sound during the fall. This local hangout of Bellingham hikers is also home to some great trails traversing the long ridge. Cedar Lake is one of the mountain's best lakes, a small, quiet swimming hole on the mountain's northeastern end. From the lake, an optional side trail climbs to viewpoints of Mount Baker and the San Juan Islands. Cedar Lake is as popular a hike in the winter as in the summer. Fall ushers in the brilliant color of the many broad-leafed trees that make up the lower forest. In winter and spring, Cedar Lake makes a great alternative to the snow-bound trails of the Cascades.

From the trailhead, Pine and Cedar Lakes Trail makes a steady ascent along an old logging road shaded by large red alder and big-leaf maple. The tread is wide, flat, and poses no obstacles. The only difficulty is the taxing, steep grade. Young kids (eight-years-old and under) might find the grade to be too difficult, but older children will probably find it to be enjoyable. At one mile, the trail reaches a three-way signed intersection. Take a left on newly built trail through the hike's only section of virgin forest. The machine-gun holes of woodpeckers are familiar sights in the bark of many trees. Another signed junction appears out of nowhere (1.3 miles)—continue straight ahead on Pine and Cedar Lakes Trail.

The climbing is over when Pine and Cedar Lakes Trail reaches a third signed junction at the ridge's crest (1.6 miles). Turn left and soon encounter the fourth signed junction for Pine or Cedar Lakes (1.8 miles). Turn left—Cedar Lake Trail quickly drops to the waters of Cedar Lake. The screech of an eagle may be in the air, or deer may be grazing the lakeshore. The lake is a favorite swimming and fishing hole of area locals. Several primitive campsites ring the lake for hikers interested in an overnight stay.

Options
Sandwiched between the Cascades and Puget Sound, Chuckanut Mountain is rich with good views. Unfortunately, forest obscures any views from Cedar Lake. To reach views of Mount Baker and the San Juan Islands, hike on the side trail signed "Scenic Overlook" on the east end of the lake. The trail steeply climbs 300 feet to a pair of overlooks (0.4 mile from Cedar Lake) atop a wooded butte. To the east, look down to Cedar Lake and north to Mount Baker. On the west side, count the San Juan Islands and scope the Olympic skyline.

Directions
From Seattle, drive north on I-5 to Exit 246, North Lake Samish. At the end of the off-ramp, turn right, cross over the freeway, and immediately turn right on Old Samish Road. Drive three miles to the signed parking lot and trailhead on the left.

Information and Contact
This area is accessible year-round. This trail is open to hikers and leashed dogs. Permits are not required—parking and access are free. For a topographic map, ask the USGS for Bellingham South. For more information, contact Whatcom County Parks and Recreation, 3373 Mount Baker Highway, Bellingham, WA 98226, 360/733-2900.

2 FRAGRANCE LAKE
Chuckanut Mountain

Level: Easy/Moderate   **Total Distance:** 4.6 miles

Hiking Time: 2.5 hours   **Elevation Gain:** 1,000 feet

Summary: A popular hike, best in the off-season, up the side of Chuckanut Mountain to a quiet wooded lake.

As far as hiking goes, summertime is best spent in the high subalpine terrain of the Cascade Mountains during its short window of accessibility. Fall, winter, and spring, also known in Seattle as Those Nine Months of Rain, have their ideal trails too, and Fragrance Lake is one of them. This popular trail is an easy to moderate climb to the forested lake that can be hiked by the whole family. Located on the north end of Chuckanut Mountain, the hike lies within the rain shadow of the Olympic Peninsula, meaning it receives about half the rain of the Seattle area. That makes Fragrance Lake an appealing destination in the fall or spring, not to mention winter, when high-country trails are covered in snow.

The trail to Fragrance Lake gains about 1,000 feet in just under two miles. That's a steady incline, one that can have you catching your breath but is not excessively difficult. With regular breaks and encouragement, young kids should be able to reach Fragrance Lake. Considering the trail's popularity, the tread is in good condition and receives regular maintenance from the Parks Department.

From the trailhead on Chuckanut Drive, signed Fragrance Lake Trail crosses an unused gravel road and begins a steady ascent up the mountain. The forest was logged more than 100 years ago but is now home to some of the biggest second-growth forest around. Douglas firs and western red cedars comprise the shady canopy. The hike's only junction (0.8 mile) is a must-see side trip—the level trail wanders 0.2 mile to a scenic lookout of the Olympics and San Juan Islands, the hike's only vista. Fragrance Lake Trail continues from the junction up the hillside. Switchbacks loop back and forth between large cedars hollowed out by fire. The trail passes through a gate blocking bicycles from the trail (1.7 miles) and drops slightly to Fragrance Lake (1.8 miles). Quiet forest surrounds the lakeshore with several good places to hop in for a swim. A 0.4-mile trail rings the lake and is recommended—tall cliffs on the east side of the lake sport cedars growing straight out of the rock.

Options
Spanning an area from the shores of Puget Sound to the crest of Chuckanut Mountain, Larrabee State Park is a treasure for hikers. There are two great side trips from Chuckanut Drive to Puget Sound: trails to Clayton Beach and Teddy Bear Cove (each about a half mile round-trip) drop to the sandy shores of Chuckanut Bay and Puget Sound. The white sand beaches are strewn with boulders and driftwood. Teddy Bear Cove trailhead is located on the left side of Chuckanut Drive, three miles past Fragrance Lake trailhead. Clayton Beach trailhead is located on the left side of Chuckanut Drive, two miles before Fragrance Lake trailhead.

Directions
From Seattle, drive north on I-5 to Chuckanut Drive (Exit 231). Turn left (west) and drive 14.5 miles to the park entrance. The signed trailhead is on the right, opposite the entrance. Park in the large, graveled pull-outs on the right side of the road before and after the trailhead.

Information and Contact
This area is accessible year-round. This trail is open to hikers and leashed dogs. A $5 day-use fee is required to park here and is payable at the trailhead, or you can get an annual State Parks Pass for $50; contact Washington State Parks and Recreation, 360/902-8500. For a topographic map, ask the USGS for Bellingham South. For more information, contact Larrabee State Park, 245 Chuckanut Drive, Bellingham, WA 98226, 360/676-2093.

3 PADILLA BAY SHORE TRAIL
Padilla Bay National Estuarine Research Reserve

Level: Easy   **Total Distance:** 4.2 miles

Hiking Time: 2 hours   **Elevation Gain:** None

Summary: Walking along the top of a large agricultural dike, this is an easy opportunity to see lots of wildlife.

Padilla Bay Shore Trail is of a different flavor than most in our region. Forsaking the mountains, this hike walks along the top of a dike on the southeastern shore of Padilla Bay. As a part of the Padilla Bay National Estuarine Research Reserve, this is a unique place. Tides recede to reveal large mud flats, and wildlife is easily spied. This is an excellent fall hike, when flocks of birds are passing through and clear skies reveal views of Mount Baker and the Olympics.

Padilla Bay Shore Trail is flat, level, and easily hiked by all. The surface is hard, compacted gravel, making it accessible to wheelchair users and families with strollers. The trail is also open to bicycles. From the trailhead, the route follows the top of a dike constructed to create farmland out of marsh. The trail crosses several sloughs, including No-Name (0.5 miles) and Indian Slough (1.3 miles).

Today the reserve covers more than 11,000 acres, and the area is flourishing as bird habitat. Thousands of migrating marsh- and shorebirds stop through the reserve during the spring and fall. Binoculars or a camera with a zoom lens are essentials. The area is also important habitat for many marine animals. Puget Sound orca pods are commonly seen in the bay during these same seasons.

The trail follows Indian Slough to a southern trailhead (2.1 miles), the turnaround spot. Views of the Olympics and even Mount Baker can be had while enjoying the salty marine air of Puget Sound. This stretch of trail is an

Padilla Bay Shore Trail is a perfect hike for families.

ideal spot to watch great blue herons feeding during low tide. An old barn is a testament to days gone by. Open year-round, Padilla Bay makes a great place to stretch the legs during winter.

Options
The trail features a wheelchair-accessible parking spot at the end of the trail, located 1.5 miles farther down Bayview-Edison Road. Wheelchair users need to check out a key at Breazeale Interpretive Center, which accesses the gate at this trailhead.

Directions
From Seattle, drive north on I-5 to Highway 20 (Exit 230). Turn left (west) and drive five miles to Farm to Market Road. Turn right (north) and drive two miles to Josh Wilson Road then turn left and drive one mile to Bayview-Edison Road. Turn left and drive to Second Street in Bay View (it is signed for Shore Trail parking). Turn left and drive one block to the parking area on the left. To reach the trail, walk back down to Bayview-Edison Road and walk 100 yards to the left—the signed trail is on the water to the right.

Information and Contact
This area is accessible year-round. This trail is open to hikers and bicyclists—dogs are not allowed in the refuge. Permits are not required. Parking and access

are free. Maps of the trail system are posted at trailheads. For a topographic map, ask the USGS for La Conner. For more information, contact Padilla Bay National Estuarine Research Reserve, 10441 Bayview-Edison Road, Mount Vernon, WA 98273, 360/428-1558.

4 LIGHTHOUSE POINT   BEST

Deception Pass State Park, on Fidalgo Island

🏢 🦌 🐕 👫

Level: Easy   **Total Distance:** 1.5 miles

Hiking Time: 1.5 hours   **Elevation Gain:** 150 feet

Summary: A short, easy loop to Lighthouse Point, a dramatic setting on Deception Pass.

Deception Pass State Park is unquestionably one of Washington's most beautiful. Set on a narrow pass between Fidalgo and Whidbey Islands, the park has miles of Puget Sound shoreline. Its most famous landmark is the bridge connecting the two islands 185 feet above the water. Many trails cross the park, and the hike to Lighthouse Point is one of the best. The trail follows Bowman Bay and explores Lighthouse Point, a rocky spit jutting into the sound. There is no better view in the park.

This hike is good for families because it's short and doesn't gain much elevation. Children can definitely hike the trail, but keep them on a short leash. There are several steep drop-offs of 100 feet or more, and accidents happen all too frequently. A great aspect of this hike is that any season is a good time to hit the trail. Shielded by the Olympic Mountains' rain shadow, the park experiences drier, sunnier weather than Seattle and never sees snow. Spring and early summer is whale season and there are plenty of opportunities to spot them from this trail, so binoculars are highly recommended.

There's not a dull moment on this hike. From the parking lot at the Bowman Bay Boat Launch, walk left along the bay and past the play fields on a gravel trail. On the right is a long pier out into Bowman Bay (0.1 mile), frequently packed with anglers. The trail makes a quick ascent (75 feet) over a rocky cliff. This is the first of many good viewpoints. After dropping back near the shore, the trail hits a junction (0.2 mile). Take a right and drop to the rocky beach connecting Fidalgo Island and Lighthouse Point.

LIGHTHOUSE POINT

INTERPRETIVE CENTER · Pass Lake · Start/Finish · Bowman Bay · PICNIC AREA · 20 · To Oak Harbor · Lighthouse Point · 0   100 yds · 0   100 m

© AVALON TRAVEL PUBLISHING, INC.

The beach separates two small coves. This is a common place to spot sea otters, great blue herons, and bald eagles. Walk onto the point (0.4 mile) and stay to the left as Lighthouse Point Trail works around the left side of the island in full view of Deception Pass. At the far end of Lighthouse Point is an adventurous option: The far end of the point is separated by a small rocky beach. To reach the end of Lighthouse Point and the lighthouse structure, climb the 30-foot ladder to get over the steep cliffs. This is the one section definitely not for children. At 0.6 mile, the trail reaches an unsigned junction. To the right is the route back to the starting point of this section of the trail. Stay left and hike to the highest spot on Lighthouse Point and its best view (0.7 mile). To return, walk back to that last unsigned junction and follow that trail as it traverses the spine of Lighthouse Point back to the first narrow beach.

Directions

From Seattle, drive north on I-5 to Highway 20 in Mount Vernon. Drive west 15 miles on Highway 20 toward Oak Harbor. Turn right on Rosario Road, immediately after Pass Lake and one mile before the Deception Pass Bridge. Take the first left into Bowman Bay and drive 0.3 mile to a stop sign. Turn left toward the boat launch and park in the large parking lot.

Information and Contact

This area is accessible year-round. This trail is open to hikers and leashed dogs. A $5 day-use fee is required to park here and is payable at the trailhead, or you can get an annual State Parks Pass for $50; contact Washington State Parks and Recreation, 360/902-8500. Maps of the trail system are available at trailheads. For a topographic map, ask the USGS for Deception Pass. For more information, contact Deception Pass State Park, Highway 20, Oak Harbor, WA 98277, 360/675-2417.

5 WEST BEACH TO GOOSE ROCK

Deception Pass State Park, on northern Whidbey Island

Level: Easy/Moderate

Hiking Time: 2 hours

Total Distance: 3.4 miles

Elevation Gain: 350 feet

Summary: A stroll along Puget Sound's best beach up to a great viewpoint atop one of Whidbey Island's highest points.

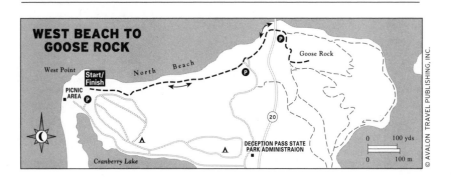

Deception Pass State Park is undoubtedly one of Washington's finest. Straddling the narrow passage between Fidalgo and Whidbey Islands, the park features miles of beach and outstanding forests. This hike takes advantage of both, running along North Beach before climbing to Goose Rock Summit, one of Whidbey's highest vantage points. Deception Pass is a very popular destination in the summer—it sometimes feels more like the mall than wilderness. The off season is a great time too because the park lies in the rain shadow of the Olympic Mountains and thus receives about half the rain of Seattle.

North Beach Trail begins near the amphitheater and quickly drops down to the beach. This is one of Puget Sound's nicest beaches. Driftwood lines the sandy shoreline and bald eagles and great blue herons regularly grace the sky. A large rock juts out into the beach (0.6 mile). If the tide is up, a small, obvious trail makes a detour around it on land. The constantly changing tide creates a strong current through Deception Pass–from the beach it looks much like a river. The beach ends around the North Beach Parking Lot, and a trail to the lot is apparent (0.9 mile).

From the parking lot, follow signs for Deception Pass bridge on Goose Rock Perimeter Trail. This is a great section of forest, with big Douglas firs and cedars providing shade. The trail climbs to the bridge along the open

The forests of Deception Pass State Park connect to West Beach.

bluff. Although the trail is lined with handrails, do not venture too close to the edge, as it can still be dangerous.

The trail passes under the bridge and splits (1.2 miles). Take Goose Rock Summit Trail and climb steadily but quickly to the bald summit (1.7 miles). From up here, much of Whidbey Island is visible to the south, including jets taking off from Whidbey Naval Station. From North Beach to the view atop Goose Rock, this is one of our area's most diverse and wonderful hikes.

Options

For a slightly longer hike (an extra 1.2 miles), Goose Rock Perimeter Trail is a great option. From the junction on the east side of the bridge, remain on Goose Rock Perimeter Trail as it winds clockwise around the summit. The trail spends time on high bluffs overlooking Cornet Bay and several small islands.

Folks looking to spend a night at Deception Pass State Park will be glad to know that it is home to a large campground. Some sites have hookups, but most are primitive. Sites fill up quickly during the summer, especially on holiday weekends.

Directions

From Seattle, drive north on I-5 to Highway 20 in Mount Vernon. Drive west 18 miles on Highway 20 toward Oak Harbor. The main entrance is located 0.5 mile after Deception Pass Bridge. Turn right into the main entrance and follow signs to West Beach. The trailhead is located at the north end of the parking lot, near the amphitheater. Trail maps are available at the entrance.

Information and Contact

This area is accessible year-round. This trail is open to hikers and leashed dogs. A $5 day-use fee is required to park here and is payable at the trailhead, or you can get an annual State Parks Pass for $50; contact Washington State Parks and Recreation, 360/902-8500. Maps of the trail system are available at trailheads. For a topographic map, ask the USGS for Deception Pass. For more information, contact Deception Pass State Park, Highway 20, Oak Harbor, WA 98277, 360/675-2417.

6 BLUFF LOOP

BEST (

Fort Ebey State Park, on Whidbey Island

🏕 ⛰ 🐴 👫

Level: Easy

Total Distance: 3.2 miles

Hiking Time: 2 hours

Elevation Gain: 400 feet

Summary: This loop explores several great trails in Fort Ebey, wandering quiet forests to high bluffs with expansive views of Puget Sound.

Once an important part of Seattle's protection from attack in World War II, Fort Ebey today enjoys a more peaceful character. Located high atop a bluff overlooking Puget Sound, the state park is teeming with miles of trail. This loop hike makes a full tour of the park, from old-growth timber on Granpa Tree Trail to views of the Olympic Mountains across the Strait of Juan de Fuca.

Fort Ebey is often overlooked by the crowds of day-trippers visiting nearby Deception Pass. Other than the occasional mountain biker, solitude is likely on these trails. Another big plus of Whidbey Island is its location within the Olympic rain shadow. Like an enormous windbreak, the Olympic Mountains absorb the blows of rainy weather, leaving sunny, dry weather to the leeward side. The rain gauge proves the phenomenon: Fort Ebey receives half the rainfall of Seattle.

It's a good idea to pick up a free map of the trails at the ranger station on the way in. This loop begins on the Pacific Northwest Trail (P.N.T.) as it climbs to a junction above Lake Pondilla (0.3 mile). Turn right onto the roadbed and make a left soon after on signed Kyle's Kettle Trail. This trail climbs when signed Granpa Tree Trail cuts to the left (0.4 mile). Take this left and drop to an enormous Douglas fir (0.6 mile). Granpa Tree Trail climbs back to a junction with Kyle's Kettle Trail (0.8 mile). Turn left onto signed Kyle's

Kettle Trail as it wanders through a forest understory of giant oceanspray and rhododendron bushes.

The route crosses a paved road and becomes Raider Creek Trail (1.2 miles), which gently climbs to signed Campground Trail (1.6 miles). Beware of the stinging nettle in this section. A quick swipe of the tall weed with your hand or leg will be felt for hours. A right on Campground Trail quickly arrives at Forest Run Trail (1.7 miles). Turn left on Forest Run Trail, then turn right on Kettles Trail (1.9 miles) and left on Hokey-Ka-Dodo Trail (2.0 miles), which finally arrives at Bluff Trail (2.2 miles), the climax of the trip.

Bluff Trail runs along the crest of the bluff overlooking the Strait of Juan de Fuca, the main shipping route from Seattle to the Pacific. Lucky hikers may see a pod of orcas in the water below. Twisted trees line the hillside and bear testament to the near-constant wind here. A windbreaker or fleece is a good thing to have here in any season.

Bluff Trail reaches Battery 248 (2.6 miles), where two large cannon emplacements stood guard over the strait in World War II. Together with similar emplacements at Fort Worden and Fort Casey, these cannons formed a "Triangle of Fire" across the strait. Fortunately, the invasion never arrived. From Battery 248, Bluff Trail drops through forest to a small machine-gun bunker and shipping beacon (3.0 miles) before arriving back at the parking lot.

From Fort Ebey, views of the Olympic Mountains across the Strait of Juan de Fuca are spectacular.

Options

Fort Ebey shares a long border with Kettles County Park to the east. Together, the two parks boast more than 28 miles of trail. This is a popular stomping ground for mountain bikers.

Fort Ebey also has a large campground with more than 50 sites. The campground is a popular summer destination but usually fills up only on weekends or holidays.

Directions

From Seattle, drive north on I-5 to Exit 189, Highway 526. Drive west five miles and follow signs to Mukilteo Ferry Terminal. Take a Washington State Ferry to the town of Clinton, on Whidbey Island. From Clinton, drive north 30 miles on Highway 525 to Libby Road. Turn left (west) and drive one mile to Valley Drive. Turn left and drive 0.3 mile to the signed entrance into the park on the right. Pass the ranger station and turn right, toward the picnic area. The road drops to the beach and turns sharply to the right, to the picnic area. Day parking is allowed here, on the outside curve in front of the beach. The signed trail begins on the inside of the curve.

Information and Contact

This hike is accessible year-round. This trail is open to hikers, leashed dogs, and mountain bikes. A $5 day-use fee is required to park here and is payable at the trailhead, or you can get an annual State Parks Pass for $50; contact Washington State Parks and Recreation, 360/902-8500. Maps of the trail system are available at the ranger station. For a topographic map, ask the USGS for Port Townsend North. For more information, contact Fort Ebey State Park, 395 Fort Ebey Road, Coupeville, WA 98239, 360/678-4636.

7 RIDGE LOOP TRAIL
South Whidbey State Park, on Whidbey Island

Level: Easy

Total Distance: 1.9 miles

Hiking Time: 1.5 hours

Elevation Gain: 300 feet

Summary: A quiet loop through old-growth forest at one of Whidbey Island's better parks.

South Whidbey State Park remains less known than its sister parks to the north, Fort Ebey and Deception Pass, but its trails are as good as any on the island. Ridge Loop Trail explores the upper reaches of the park, which is situated on a bluff high above Puget Sound. Much of the hike wanders through old forests untouched by the saw or ax, meaning there are numerous big trees to take your breath away.

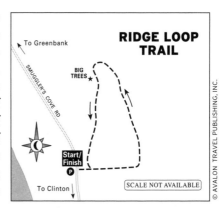

If you would prefer to avoid the crowds, South Whidbey State Park is the place to hike. In fact, if you would like to avoid winter's wet weather, South Whidbey Island State Park is again a good refuge. This part of the island sees roughly half the annual rainfall of Seattle. With two of hikers' biggest headaches out of the picture, South Whidbey's appeal is obvious.

Begin the hike by crossing Smuggler's Cove Road and entering the forest at the Wilbert trailhead. Ridge Loop Trail is signed and proceeds straight ahead, while Wilbert Trail turns to the left. From this junction, Ridge Loop Trail gently climbs through an old forest of fir, hemlock, and cedar. The trees grow in size as the hike meanders through the forest. Don't be surprised to encounter woodpeckers, deer, or other friendly wildlife. The grade is never difficult, and children should not have a challenging time.

After passing through a picturesque stand of alder, with skinny trunks of white and red bark shooting to the sky, the trail reaches an old roadbed (0.7 mile). This section of trail is very level and smooth. Although it may seem as though the trail will never reach the crest of anything, the slopes eventually drop to both sides and the trail is on a small ridge.

The trail noticeably leaves the roadbed and arrives at an unsigned junction with

Wilbert Trail in the middle of a grove of enormous Douglas fir (1.3 miles). To the right, Wilbert Trail drops to several more enormous trees, both standing and fallen. This trail is a fun side trip if you want to see some more big trees. The loop hike heads to the left on Wilbert Trail, which rambles through great forest back to the trailhead (1.9 miles).

Little-known South Whidbey State Park features quiet trails.

Options

South Whidbey State Park features a pair of other short trails that are well worth mentioning. The Beach Access Trail (0.5 mile) is the most popular trail in the park. It drops from the day-use parking lot atop the bluff down to a beautiful stretch of beach nearly a mile long along Admiralty Inlet. South Discovery Trail (0.3 mile) leaves the graveled parking lot and makes a quick loop through a lush forest of big trees. The route crosses a small creek on a pair of nice bridges. Hikers with the time will enjoy adding either of these short hikes to their trip here.

The park is also home to a large campground. With access to old-growth forest and a prime stretch of Puget Sound shoreline, this is a great place to spend a summer weekend.

Directions

From Seattle, drive north on I-5 to Exit 189, Highway 526. Drive west five miles and follow signs to Mukilteo Ferry Terminal. Take a Washington State Ferry to the town of Clinton, on Whidbey Island. From Clinton, drive north 11 miles on Highway 525 to Bush Point Road. Turn left and drive five miles (as the road becomes Smuggler's Cove Road) to the park entrance on the left. Park in the gravel lot, immediately to the left upon entering. The signed trailhead is directly across Smuggler's Cove Road.

Information and Contact

This area is accessible year-round. This trail is open to hikers and leashed dogs. A $5 day-use fee is required to park here and is payable at the trailhead, or you can get an annual State Parks Pass for $50; contact Washington State Parks and Recreation, 360/902-8500. A map of the trail system is posted at the trailhead. For a topographic map, ask the USGS for Freeland. For more information, contact South Whidbey State Park, 4128 Smuggler's Cove Road, Freeland, WA 98249, 360/331-4559.

8 DE LEO WALL LOOP
Cougar Mountain Regional Wildland Park

🎖 🏇 🚻

Level: Easy

Hiking Time: 2 hours

Total Distance: 4.0 miles

Elevation Gain: 450 feet

Summary: A rambling loop along the western slopes of Cougar Mountain to a small viewpoint.

De Leo Wall Loop is the closest hike to Seattle of the many listings in this book. With a trailhead located just minutes from I-90 and I-405, hitting the trail is quick and painless. This hike merges several trails located in the western portion of Cougar Mountain Regional Park for an easy, fun hike. De Leo Wall itself is not much to shake a stick at; the view is unimpressive and getting smaller each year. But the hike as a whole is a quiet trip through Cougar Mountain's notable forests.

As the shortest member of the Issaquah Alps, Cougar Mountain rarely attracts much fanfare. But the park and its trails, especially De Leo Wall Loop, have numerous advantages. First, it's rare that these trails see snow. Thus, there is hiking in every season, no matter the weather in the Cascades. Second, De Leo Wall Loop is a great trip for kids. The elevation change is minimal and seeing wildlife such as deer, coyotes, or woodpeckers is not out of the question.

This hike begins at Red Town trailhead, Cougar Mountain's most popular trailhead. The route follows Wildside Trail for the first 0.7 mile, crossing a pair of creeks on wooden bridges. Throughout this first segment, numerous trails intersect the route at signed junctions–simply stick to Wildside Trail.

Wildside Trail reaches a junction with Marshall Hill Trail (0.7 mile), where the route turns right on Marshall Hill and gently climbs through a valley of ferns. The trail circles around the summit of Marshall Hill and crosses a paved access road (1.8 miles), where it becomes De Leo Wall Trail. The trail drops suddenly to De Leo Wall (2.3 miles). Here, Pacific madrone and Douglas fir are gradually blocking the view to the southeast.

De Leo Wall Trail wanders through quiet, shady forest on its way to a junction with Wildside Trail (2.8 miles). This stretch of trail can be lonely and quiet on a summer's day, let alone on a drizzly winter morning. At the junction with Wildside Trail, bear left. Wildside Trail parallels the upper reaches of Coal Creek as it wanders back to Red Town trailhead (4 miles).

Options

A worthwhile side trip is Ford Slope Mine Shaft. The old remains of the mine, including the sealed mine

De Leo Wall Loop is a good trail for families with small children.

shaft, are located immediately off of Wildside Trail, at a signed junction 0.3 mile from Red Town trailhead. Signboards are posted with historic pictures of the mine in operation, with many shots taken from exactly where hikers are standing.

Directions

From Seattle, drive east on I-90 to Exit 13. When the exit ramp splits, bear right toward Lakemount. Turn right onto Lakemount Boulevard and drive three miles to the Red Town trailhead on the left, as Lakemount Boulevard curves sharply to the right.

Information and Contact

This area is accessible year-round. This trail is open to hikers, leashed dogs, and horses. No permits are required—parking and access are free. A map of the trail system is posted at the trailhead. For a topographic map, ask the USGS for Bellevue South. For more information, contact King County Parks and Recreation, 18201 Southeast Cougar Mountain Drive, Bellevue, WA 98006, 206/296-4232.

9 ANTI-AIRCRAFT PEAK
Cougar Mountain Regional Wildland Park

Level: Easy

Hiking Time: 2 hours

Total Distance: 3.5 miles

Elevation Gain: 300 feet

Summary: This easy hike uses several trails as it rambles along the upper slopes of Cougar Mountain.

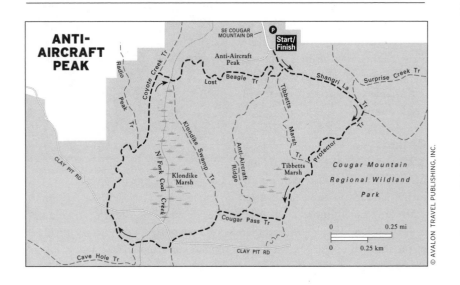

Just 20 minutes from downtown Seattle, this loop on Anti-Aircraft Peak is one of the area's most accessible trails. Yet, surprisingly, it can be refreshingly lonely on most days. This route follows several lightly used trails as they wander through Cougar Mountain's great forests. With little elevation change, this hike is ideal for kids. Runners get a kick out of it too; Cougar Mountain is a favorite training park for runners, and it is home to several trail running races in the summer.

Anti-Aircraft Peak gets its name from the placement of large guns in World War II, designed to shoot down invading airplanes. Later, they were replaced by Minuteman missiles in the heat of the Cold War. The hike starts from the parking lot on Shangri-La Trail, an old roadbed. Turn right at a signed junction for Protector Trail (0.6 mile). This short trail soon hits Tibbetts Marsh Trail (0.9 mile). King County has done a great job of maintaining the trails. Although there are some muddy spots, much of the trail is in excellent condi-

© SCOTT LEONARD

The lush forests of Cougar Mountain also function as a training park for runners, and are home to several trail running races in the summer.

tion. Directionally challenged hikers will be glad to know that all of the junctions along the route are well signed, virtually eliminating the possibility of getting lost.

Big-leaf maples and red alders provide much of the forest canopy, while green sword ferns cover the forest floor. Turn left on Tibbetts Marsh Trail as it clears a hump and reaches Cougar Pass Trail (1.2 miles). Turn right onto Cougar Pass Trail. Anti-Aircraft Ridge Trail takes off to the right (1.4 miles), and soon thereafter Klondike Swamp Trail does the same (1.5 miles). Stay to the left and follow Cougar Pass Trail to a junction with Coyote Creek Trail (1.7 miles), where a paved road crosses the route.

Cross the road and follow Coyote Creek Trail to the right. This is the best part of the route, where the forest is filled with salmonberry and salal, and every tree gathers moss. Deer are frequently seen throughout these quiet forests. Circling Klondike Marsh, Coyote Creek Trail reaches a junction with Lost Beagle Trail (2.8 miles). Turn right and endure the hike's only section of switchbacks, which casually climb the gentle ridge. Stay to the left as Lost Beagle Trail passes junctions for Klondike Swamp Trail (2.9 miles), Anti-Aircraft Ridge Trail (3.5 miles), and Tibbetts Marsh Trail (3.5 miles) on the way back to the trailhead.

Directions

From Seattle, drive east on I-90 to Exit 13. When the exit ramp splits, bear right toward Lakemount. Turn right onto Lakemount Boulevard and drive 2.5 miles to SE Cougar Mountain Way. Turn left and drive 1.2 miles to SE Cougar Mountain Drive, on the right. Veer right and drive one mile to where the road emerges in a large parking lot. The signed trailhead is on the left, in front of the caretaker's house.

Information and Contact

This area is accessible year-round. This trail is open to hikers, leashed dogs, and horses. No permits are required—parking and access are free. A map of the trail system is posted at the trailhead. For a topographic map, ask the USGS for Bellevue South. For more information, contact King County Parks and Recreation, 18201 Southeast Cougar Mountain Drive, Bellevue, WA 98006, 206/296-4232.

10 SQUAK MOUNTAIN
Squak Mountain State Park

BEST ◖

🦌 🔵 🐾 👫

Level: Easy/Moderate

Hiking Time: 3.5 hours

Total Distance: 6.6 miles

Elevation Gain: 1,680 feet

Summary: The hidden gem of the Issaquah Alps, Squak Mountain offers a quiet forest hike in any season.

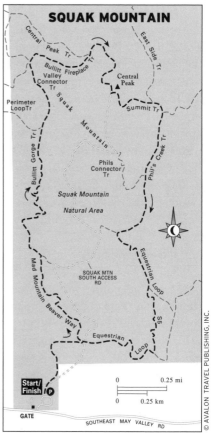

Of the four mountains that make up the Issaquah Alps–Rattlesnake, Tiger, Squak, and Cougar–Squak Mountain remains the least known of the group. The few hikers who regularly visit these quiet trails share a geographical joke about the origin of the mountain's name: If you were stuck between a tiger and a cougar, you'd squak too. All jokes aside, the trip to Squak's summit is one full of surprises, from lush fern valleys to unexpected wildlife. The trail system is lightly used, so it's okay to expect lonely trails. Best of all, Squak is a great visit year-round, sporting a different feel in every season.

This southern route to the summit uses numerous trails in the park's network, which can be confusing. Many junctions are unsigned and reveal little clue as to where they lead. A map is highly recommended before hitting the trail—without one, it might be a long day of wandering.

Beginning from the parking lot, the route crosses South Access Road and faces two trails. To the left is Thomas Interpretive Trail (0.3 mile), an educational loop featuring signboards. Take the right trail, a new trail yet to be named. It climbs gently to a junction (0.5 mile). Head left on Mad Mountain Beaver Way Trail, where the trail leads through a hardwood forest of maple and alder. When the route reaches another junction (1.2 miles), turn left on Bullitt Gorge Trail, climbing very steeply to a fork (2.0 miles). Bear left, continuing on Bullitt Gorge Trail to a signed junction with Perimeter Loop Trail (2.3 miles). Bear right on Valley Connector Trail to Bullitt Fireplace Trail (2.7 miles).

Turn right and soon come to the site of the old Bullitt Fireplace on the right (2.9 miles). This impressive hearth is left over from the Bullitt Family, who had a cabin here in the early 20th century. The trail quickly drops elevation to a junction with Central Peak Trail (3.2 miles). Bear right and make the final climb to Squak's summit, at 2,024 feet elevation (3.5 miles). Trees have grown

Squak Mountain has many quiet sections of forest.

up around much of the summit, which is home to an array of imposing microwave radio towers. The last remaining view through the trees is a good one of downtown Seattle.

The hike down from the summit follows many rarely used trails that see little brushing or other maintenance. Encounters with wildlife should be no surprise, from bald eagles roosting in tall firs to deer grazing on a forest floor covered in ferns. From the summit, walk down the South Access Road 100 yards to Summit Trail C6, turn left, and leave the road. The route drops quickly, to Squak Trail S3 (3.8 miles). Turn right and continue dropping to another junction (4.2 miles). Stay to the left, hiking on Phil's Creek Trail (4.2 miles) to Equestrian Loop Trail (4.6 miles). Turn left and drop to a signed junction (5.2 miles). Turn right on S5 and reencounter Equestrian Loop (5.6 miles). Turn right and cross a very impressive bridge spanning Phil's Creek (5.8 miles). Much of the route is edged by salmonberries, which usually ripen in June. The trail continues and crosses South Access Road (6.2 miles). Here, you'll recognize a junction from the beginning of the hike. Turn left and drop to the parking lot (6.6 miles).

Options

For an easier hike tailored for young children, explore the route backwards and only up to the bridge crossing Phil's Creek. This 1.8-mile hike features less climbing, a nice forest, and a stream.

Directions

From Seattle, drive east on I-90 to State Route 900 at Exit 15. Turn right and drive west four miles on SR-900 to May Valley Road. Turn left and drive 2.2 miles to the signed parking lot for Squak Mountain State Park, on the left.

Information and Contact

This trail is accessible year-round and is open to hikers, leashed dogs, and horses. No wheelchair access. A $5 day-use fee is required to park here and is payable at the trailhead, or you can get an annual State Parks Pass for $50; contact Washington State Parks and Recreation, 360/902-8500. For a topographic map, ask Green Trails for No. 203S, Cougar Mountain/Squak Mountain, or ask the USGS for Bellevue South. For more information, contact Washington State Parks and Recreation, P.O. Box 42650, Olympia, WA 98504-2669, 360/902-8844.

11 BIG TREE LOOP

BEST 🌙

Tiger Mountain State Forest

🏊 🐎 👫

Level: Easy

Hiking Time: 2 hours

Total Distance: 2.8 miles

Elevation Gain: 100 feet

Summary: Kids love this easy hike through a lost grove of old, large trees-the best forest on Tiger Mountain.

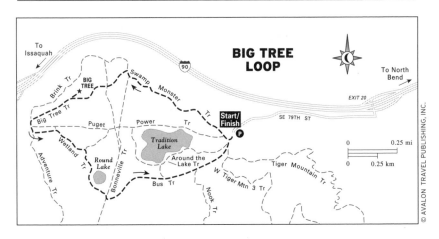

This hike makes for one of the best child-friendly hikes in the Seattle area. This route makes use of several trails on Tradition Plateau, located along the lower north side of Tiger Mountain. Big Tree is but the largest of several attractions along the way. This hike is great for hikers of all abilities since there is little elevation change. A portion of this loop is wheelchair accessible—Bus Trail and Around the Lake Trail have been refurbished to meet ADA standards. There are no signs in the section of the loop from the Brink Trail to the Wetland Trail—a Green Trails map is recommended to avoid confusion.

Beginning in the High Point parking lot, head west on the road beneath the power lines, walking downhill. Within 20 yards you'll see the signed entrance to the Swamp Monster Trail. Swamp Monster Trail winds down the hillside to a large wetland surrounded by forest. Instead of detouring, the trail heads straight into the swamp. Don't worry, for this section of trail features lots of well-constructed boardwalk, keeping feet dry. Several signboards are also posted, weaving forest education into a children's story.

Swamp Monster Trail emerges from the swamp and quickly passes beneath two sets of power lines (0.6 mile) before again entering the forest on signed Big

Small Round Lake is a great place to see wildlife and birds.

Tree Trail. Here, the forest is noticeably larger. Although it was once logged, boggy soil provided plenty of water for rapid regrowth. The granddaddy of the forest is Big Tree (1.0 mile), a 200- to 400-year-old Douglas fir spared the ax nearly 100 years ago. A picture in front of this tree—nearly 25 feet around—is easily worth a thousand words.

Where Big Tree Trail ends at Brink Trail (1.2 miles), turn left. The trail quickly reaches power lines. Cross the access road and turn left on the unsigned trail beneath the last set of lines (1.3 miles) before the trail enters the forest. The unsigned Wetland Trail cuts off to the right just a few hundred yards in. After a quick climb, Wetland Trail hits a junction with an unsigned feeder trail (1.7 miles). Stay to the right on Wetland Trail as it delves into its namesake and finds Round Lake (1.9 miles). Ducks and other migrating birds are frequent visitors to this quiet watering hole. Wetland Trail crosses beneath another set of power lines (2.0 miles) and becomes Bus Trail. Quiet at first, this easy trail gains a lot of visitors when it encounters a rusted-out, abandoned bus in the forest (2.4 miles). From there, Bus Trail heads back to the parking lot (2.8 miles).

Options

Wheelchair users will be happy to learn that a portion of this hike is wheelchair accessible. Bus Trail and Around the Lake Trail have been refurbished to meet ADA standards. Together they form a one-mile loop that wanders from the south shores of Tradition Lake to lush, green forest. The entire route is flat and well-graveled, with no elevation gain.

Directions

From Seattle, drive east on I-90 to High Point, Exit 20, just east of Issaquah. From the off-ramp, turn right and quickly turn right again, onto SE 79th Street. This is the entrance to High Point trailhead, located 0.5 mile down the gravel road. When the parking lot is full (most weekends), vehicles must park below the No Parking signs, close to the I-90 off-ramp.

Information and Contact

This trail is accessible year-round and is open to hikers and leashed dogs. Permits are not required. Parking and access are free. For topographic maps, ask Green Trails for No. 204S, Tiger Mountain, or ask the USGS for Bellevue South and Fall City. For more information, contact Washington Department of Natural Resources, P.O. Box 47001, Olympia, WA 98504-7001, 360/902-1375.

12 TALUS ROCKS
Tiger Mountain State Forest

Level: Easy/Moderate

Hiking Time: 2 hours

Total Distance: 3.1 miles

Elevation Gain: 650 feet

Summary: A loop to a cluster of extremely large talus boulders in the middle of the mossy forest.

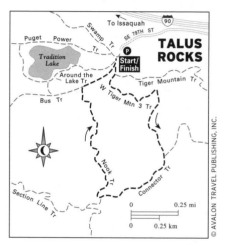

A trip to Talus Rocks makes for a fun journey on a lazy weekend afternoon. One of the best hikes on Tiger Mountain, the trail is easy enough for most kids to conquer. Wandering through a lush, green forest, it climbs to a nice waterfall and, the real draw, a group of massive boulders. The rocks are chunks of Tiger Mountain that have broken off in slides and come to rest in this spot. The rocks are so big that they created large caves beneath them, now home to numerous bats. As a whole, this hike is a great way to experience Tiger Mountain.

Beginning at High Point parking lot, find the well-graveled trail to the right of the restrooms. Around the Lake Trail and then Bus Trail quickly spur off to the right—continue straight ahead and pass through the horse/bike guard (0.1 mile) where the signed West Tiger Mountain #3 Trail begins climbing. This hike shares the trail with the crowds headed up to the summit of West Tiger Mountain #3. It is mostly old roadbed at first and is very rocky in places due to the heavy use.

This section of trail is the major elevation gain of the route. Although not difficult for most hikers, small children may find it challenging. Traveling through mossy forest of maple and fir, the trail reaches a junction with Connector Trail (0.8 mile). Turn right onto Connector Trail and leave behind the crowds headed to West Tiger #3.

Connector Trail quickly rises and dips to a great waterfall (1.0 mile), where a small stream cascades nearly 100 feet down exposed bedrock between banks of fluffy moss. Crossing the creek, Connector Trail reaches the upper portion

Talus Rocks offers a quiet trail, perfect for a lazy afternoon hike.

of Talus Rocks Loop (1.2 miles) among a party of enormous boulders. Draped in moss and supporting large fir trees, Talus Rocks are overwhelmingly big. Some of the rocks have created substantial caves beneath them, which are closed to hikers and solely reserved for the bats, although it is unlikely you'll spot the fluttering creatures.

Talus Rocks Trail makes a very short loop above, below, and around the rocks. Because of the high use this area receives year-round, it's necessary to stay off the rocks to prevent overuse and abuse. At the western end of the loop, the trail crosses a small stream and immediately comes to the signed junction with Nook Trail (1.2 miles). Turn right on Nook Trail and quickly drop down the mountainside. This section of trail features lush forest, where salmonberry, vine maple, and devil's club grow to immense sizes. The sounds of birds are never far off, from robins to downy woodpeckers to red-tailed hawks. Nook Trail winds down to the well-used and graveled Bus Trail (2.7 miles). Turn right and quickly arrive back at West Tiger Mountain #3 Trail (2.9 miles). The trailhead and parking lot are to the left.

Options

Parents with small children who are not ready for the challenge of elevation gain on this hike will want to check out Big Tree Loop (see previous listing).

Directions

From Seattle, drive east on I-90 to High Point, Exit 20, just east of Issaquah. From the off-ramp, turn right and quickly turn right again, onto SE 79th Street. This is the entrance to High Point trailhead, located 0.5 mile down the gravel road. When the parking lot is full (most weekends), vehicles must park below the No Parking signs, close to the I-90 off-ramp.

Information and Contact

This trail is accessible year-round. This trail is open to hikers and leashed dogs. Permits are not required. Parking and access are free. For topographic maps, ask Green Trails for No. 204S, Tiger Mountain, or ask the USGS for Fall City. For more information, contact Washington Department of Natural Resources, P.O. Box 47001, Olympia, WA 98504-7001, 360/902-1375.

13 WEST TIGER MOUNTAIN #3
Tiger Mountain State Forest

Level: Moderate

Hiking Time: 2.5 hours

Total Distance: 5.0 miles

Elevation Gain: 2,000 feet

Summary: A grind-it-out, catch-your-breath ascent along one of Tiger Mountain's most-traveled trails.

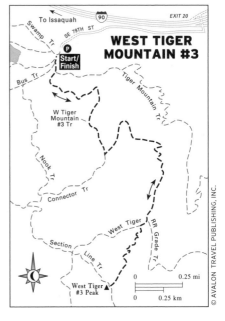

High Point trailhead at Tiger Mountain is the state's busiest. One visit on a summer weekend will quickly illustrate that fact, with cars lining the road out to I-90. But with 80 miles of trails, crowds quickly disperse into the forest. West Tiger Mountain #3 Trail remains one of the most popular hikes from this trailhead. The trail makes an all-out assault on the lowest of West Tiger Mountain's three summits. Climbing through quiet forests of maple and fir, West Tiger Mountain #3 is a conditioning favorite with runners and hikers.

Beginning from High Point parking lot, find the well-graveled trail to the right of the restrooms. Around the Lake Trail and Bus Trail quickly spur off to the right—continue straight ahead for West Tiger #3 and pass through the horse/bike guard (0.1 mile). The signed West Tiger Mountain #3 Trail now begins climbing. The trail is mostly old roadbed at first and is very rocky in places. The trail reaches a junction with Connector Trail (0.8 mile). Turn left, remaining on West Tiger #3 Trail as it continues the ascent.

The trail crosses a signed, buried cable line (1.0 mile), a recurring event over the remainder of the trail. Although it appears at times to be a usable trail, avoid it. Lacking maintenance and any layout planning, it's a poor substitute for trail. West Tiger Mountain #3 intersects West Tiger RR Grade Trail (1.8 miles) at a signed junction and continues up the hillside. Short, demanding switchbacks gain elevation quickly through this section, the most challenging of the hike. As the forest breaks and reveals a view to the east (2.4 miles), hikers will be relieved to know that they are close to the top (2.5 miles).

The summit is bald on one side, revealing far-flung vistas to the south. Seattle stands out brightly against Puget Sound. On clear days, Mount Rainier takes up much of the southern horizon. Plenty of space can be found for a relaxing snack before heading back down.

Large swaths of sword ferns are typical on Tiger Mountain.

Options

It's easy to lengthen this hike. Catch a little more elevation by hiking to West Tiger Mountain #2, a peak with an extra 250 feet in elevation. From the summit of West Tiger #3, continue hiking on the trail signed for West Tiger #2 to another great view and a total distance of 6.0 miles. Or choose a different route down, by catching Connector Trail to Talus Rocks, down to Bus Trail, for a 6.3-mile journey. Tiger Mountain's expansive trail system never gets old because it allows users to create so many different hikes.

Directions

From Seattle, drive east on I-90 to High Point, Exit 20, just east of Issaquah. From the off-ramp, turn right and quickly turn right again, onto SE 79th Street. This is the entrance to High Point trailhead, located 0.5 mile down the gravel road. When the parking lot is full (most weekends), vehicles must park below the No Parking signs, close to the I-90 off-ramp.

Information and Contact

This trail is accessible year-round and is open to hikers and leashed dogs. Permits are not required. Parking and access are free. For topographic maps, ask Green Trails for No. 204S, Tiger Mountain, or ask the USGS for Fall City. For more information, contact Washington Department of Natural Resources, P.O. Box 47001, Olympia, WA 98504-7001, 360/902-1375.

14 POINT DEFIANCE OUTSIDE PERIMETER

in Tacoma on Puget Sound

Level: Easy | **Total Distance:** 4.1 miles
Hiking Time: 2 hours | **Elevation Gain:** 100 feet

Summary: An easy loop along the cliffs of Point Defiance Park with big trees and Puget Sound views.

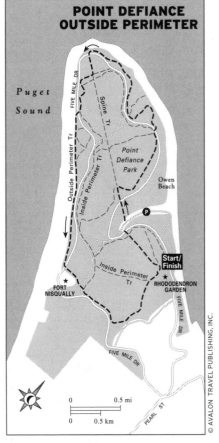

The feather in Tacoma's cap, Point Defiance is a rare respite from the noise of the city. Secluded on a large point jutting into Commencement Bay, Point Defiance lays claim to miles of waterfront and some of Puget Sound's best views. Although its exact ranking depends on who you ask, Point Defiance is unquestionably one of the largest urban parks in North America. Large conifer forests grace the Outside Perimeter Trail, a welcome change of scenery from Tacoma's industrial core. Point Defiance is also home to the city's zoo and aquarium; the roar of an elephant shouldn't be a surprise. Tacoma locals dearly love running and hiking on Point Defiance's Outside Perimeter Trail.

The park is crisscrossed by numerous trails but by far the best and most scenic route is Outside Perimeter Trail. Running along the cliffs that mark the edge of much of the park, the loop trail frequently offers views of the Tacoma Narrows far below. Hiking in the park can be a bit confusing, but nearly all the junctions are marked by signposts. The Outside Perimeter Trail is denoted by white squares on all of the three-foot-tall posts. Follow the white squares and you will know you are on the correct path. The trail has no official trailhead—this description begins at the first obvious trailhead opposite Rhododendron Garden. If parking is full, park at the zoo parking lot—the unsigned trailhead begins at the northern end of the lot.

From the trailhead at Rhododendron Garden, cross the street to the flower garden and the obvious trail. Take a right and make a counterclockwise loop around the park. At 1.1 miles you'll come to the trail's first view of the water far below. Keep a safe distance from all cliffs, which are sandy and erode easily. A large Douglas Fir, known as the Mountaineer Tree, is at 1.5 miles. At three miles you'll come to a great view of the Tacoma Narrows Bridge and its new companion in progress. Don't be surprised to run across deer, unlikely residents of the spacious park.

Options

Point Defiance features two other trails—the Inside Perimeter Trail (three miles) and the Spine Trail (two miles). These trails offer shorter routes around the park and can be utilized to make the Outside Perimeter Trail a bit shorter. Both trails are accessible from the Rhododendron Garden trailhead.

Directions

From Seattle, drive south on I-5 to Highway 16 in Tacoma. Drive west 3.5 miles on Highway 16 to the 6th Avenue/Pearl Street exit. Turn right (north) and drive four miles to the road's end at Point Defiance Park. Enter the park and follow signs for Five Mile drive. After 0.4 mile, park on the right opposite signed Rhododendron Garden. Seattle Bus routes 10 or 11 will take you to Point Defiance Park.

Information and Contact

This area is accessible year-round. This trail is open to hikers, leashed dogs, and mountain bikes. Permits are not required. Parking and access are free. Maps of the trail system are posted at trailheads. For a topographic map, ask the USGS for Gig Harbor. Or download a free trail map from the Tacoma Parks website at www.metroparkstacoma.org/page.php?id=239. For more information, contact Metro Parks Tacoma, 4702 South 19th Street, Tacoma, WA 98405, 253/305-1000.

15 BROWN FARM DIKE TRAIL   BEST €
Nisqually National Wildlife Refuge

Level: Easy   **Total Distance:** 5.0 miles

Hiking Time: 2.5 hours   **Elevation Gain:** 100 feet

Summary: An easy, scenic hike through one of Washington's most impressive wildlife refuges.

One of Western Washington's largest undisturbed estuaries, Nisqually National Wildlife Refuge is an unnoticed treasure along I-5. Here, where freshwater meets saltwater, a rich habitat exists for animals of all sorts but especially birds. Thousands of migratory birds pass through the refuge each spring and fall on their way to warmer climates or feeding grounds. Mallards, widgeons, teal, Canada geese, red-tailed hawks, and great blue heron are regular sightings. Fortunately for those of us stuck on the ground, the Brown Farm Dike Trail explores this unique area.

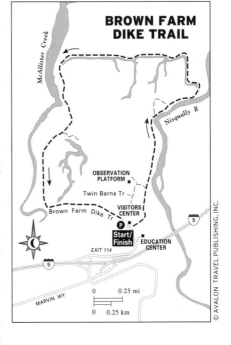

Much of the refuge is an expansive collection of marshes. The wide, slow-flowing Nisqually runs through the middle, but where the river ends and the sound begins is difficult to discern. Brown Farm Dike Trail features several viewing platforms and blinds, where visitors can spy on wildlife without being noticed. It's a good idea to bring a pair of binoculars. Be aware that a large portion of the Brown Farm Dike Trail is closed October–January to offer winged creatures a sanctuary during hunting season. The refuge has a first-rate visitors center, open Wednesday–Sunday year-round.

Brown Farm Dike Trail begins on the right (east) side of the visitors center. The trail parallels the Nisqually River as it flows into Puget Sound. At 1.2 miles is Ring Dike Trail, a short detour on the left leading to a wooden blind. It reconnects with Brown Farm Dike Trail at 1.4 miles. Brown Farm Dike

© SCOTT LEONARD

The boardwalk traverses wetlands at Nisqually National Wildlife Refuge.

Trail reaches Puget Sound (1.6 miles) and follows its shores west past a raised observation platform (1.9 miles). Brown Farm Dike Trail makes its way back along McAllister Creek and passes a short, signed trail leading to another blind (3.0 miles). The trail hits a junction with Cross Dike Trail (4.0 miles)—take a left and follow Cross Dike Trail as it returns to the visitors center.

Options
A shorter, wheelchair-accessible option is Twin Barns Trail, a one-mile loop with many interpretive signs explaining the history and ecology of the area. It's an easy, good introduction to the refuge and the animals that live here. The trail is completely built of wooden boardwalk, making it accessible to all.

Directions
From Seattle, drive south on I-5 through Tacoma to Nisqually, Exit 114. Turn right (west) onto Brown Farm Road and drive 0.3 mile to the well-signed trailhead.

Information and Contact
This area is accessible year-round. This trail is open to hikers only–dogs are not allowed in the refuge. A $3 day-use fee is required to park here and is payable at the trailhead. Maps of the trail system are available at the visitors center. For a topographic map, ask the USGS for Nisqually. For more information, contact Nisqually National Wildlife Refuge, 100 Brown Farm Road, Olympia, WA 98516, 360/753-9467.

OLYMPIC PENINSULA

© SCOTT LEONARD

BEST HIKES

◖ **Best Hikes for Viewing Wildflowers**
Mount Townsend, **page 78**

◖ **Best Kid-Friendly Hikes**
Dungeness Spit, **page 74**

Clear days in Seattle are few and far between, so

Seattleites have learned to cherish them when they happen. One of the best parts of a sunny, cloudless day is the view of the Olympic Mountains, a cousin of the Cascade Mountains across the pond of Puget Sound.

The Olympics are justifiably famous (or infamous) for the crazy amount of rain that visits the peninsula. The westside river valleys get about 140 inches a year, and the region tops out at 200 inches a year near the crest. Yes, more than 200 inches, which amounts to more than 18 vertical feet of water. There may be other, drier regions of Washington, but the Olympic Peninsula is one of the United States' most unique places.

With subalpine meadows and flowing glaciers, the Olympic Mountains are one of Washington's wildest and most beautiful ranges. Several unique species call these forests home, including Roosevelt elk, Olympic salamanders, and Olympic marmots. The park also offers some of our best chances to see black bears. Late summer in the high country is practically a bear mecca, when the sedate creatures gorge themselves into a stupor on ripe huckleberries. Wolf packs once prowled these mountains before humans wiped them out in the early 20th century. While talks of reintroduction to the area have quieted down recently, wilderness lovers can only hope for such an action.

Accessing the mountains requires taking a ferry or driving through Tacoma on the Narrows Bridge. The mountains may feel distant from Seattle, but in reality, the rugged peaks aren't more than 30 miles from downtown. Taking a ferry from Edmonds to Kingston adds extra time to the trip and consequently the trailheads are all 2.0- or 2.5-hour drives from Seattle – but these hikes are so great that it's worth the extra time.

Although the majority of the hikes in this chapter are in the Olympic Mountains, one exception to the mountain hikes is Dungeness Spit. The five-mile-long beach juts out into the Strait of Juan de Fuca and is home to one of the West Coast's oldest lighthouses. This is an ideal hike for families and wildlife enthusiasts. Mount Zion is the easiest of the mountain hikes, with a short trip to the small mountain's summit offering views of Puget Sound and the Cascades. The Mount Townsend Trail leads to two different destinations – its namesake and Silver Lakes – and offers incredible views of both Puget Sound and the Olympic Range's interior. One of this book's longest hikes, the Silver Lakes Trail, is a quiet and lightly visited path, and Big Quilcene Trail passes through outstanding forests to beautiful views at Marmot Pass. All of the hikes contained in this chapter are highly recommended – just keep in mind that the drive makes for a longer day. Of course, with great places to stay in Port Townsend, these hikes are the perfect part of a weekend getaway.

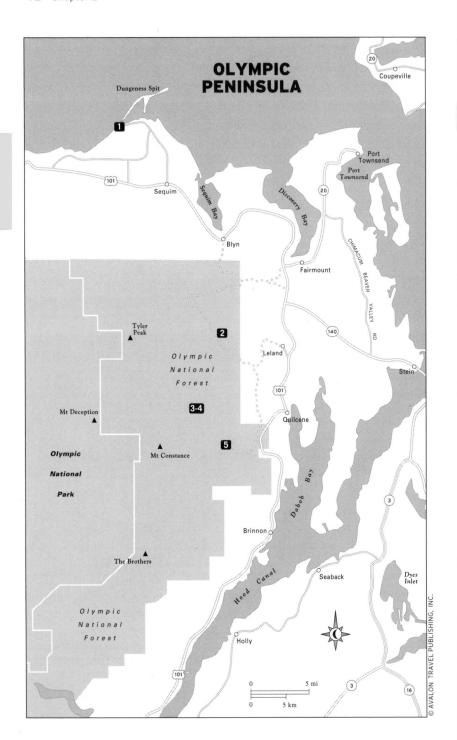

OLYMPIC PENINSULA

Dungeness Spit

Coupeville

1

Port Townsend

Port Townsend

101

Sequim

Sequim Bay

Discovery Bay

20

Blyn

Fairmount

CHIMACUM BEAVER VALLEY RD

Tyler Peak

2

140

Olympic National Forest

Leland

Stein

Mt Deception

3-4

101

Quilcene

5

Olympic National Park

Mt Constance

Dabob Bay

3

The Brothers

Brinnon

Seaback

Dyes Inlet

Olympic National Forest

Hood Canal

Holly

101

0   5 mi

0   5 km

3

16

Olympic Peninsula Hikes

1 DUNGENESS SPIT

BEST 🅲

on the northeast tip of the Olympic Peninsula

🏠 🦌 🏊 🧭 🚻

Level: Easy

Total Distance: 11.0 miles

Hiking Time: 5 hours

Elevation Gain: 150 feet

Summary: An outstanding beach hike along Dungeness Spit which juts out into the Puget Sound and culminates at a celebrated lighthouse.

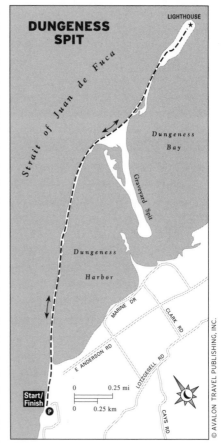

Set within Dungeness National Wildlife Refuge, Dungeness Spit is undoubtedly one of the state's premier sites to watch wildlife. This is also one of our region's best beach walks. Dungeness Spit juts into the Strait of Juan de Fuca more than five miles, creating a quiet harbor and bay of tide flats. The spit is constantly growing, being added to from nearby bluffs eroding sandy sediments into the strait. At the end of the spit stands a historic lighthouse built in 1857 and still open to the public. The refuge hosts a rich and diverse ecosystem that is home to birds, critters by land and sea, and numerous fish and shellfish.

Take note that this is one of the few hikes contained in this book that is more than two hours from Seattle. From the ferry terminal on the Kitsap Peninsula in Kingston, Dungeness Spit is about a 90-minute drive. Despite the long drive, this is a popular destination for Seattle-area day hik-ers. It is also very popular with folks vacationing on the peninsula. On any day, the trip is worth the time in the car.

The hike is less of a trail and more of a walk on a great beach. From the parking lot, the trail quickly passes through a section of forest before dropping down to the spit (0.4 mile). Before the trail drops, there are several well-built wooden viewing platforms offering a wide vista of the Strait of Juan de Fuca. After dropping to the spit, the trail proper disappears and the hike is simply a walk out along the sandy beach of Dungeness Spit. Driftwood and native grasses line the shores of the spit which is just 50 feet wide in places—it gives the feeling of walking on the seawater. The end of the hike is Dungeness Lighthouse (5.5 miles), but turning around at any point will still yield a fun trip.

The refuge sees more than 250 species of birds each year, mainly shorebirds and waterfowl, some migratory and some permanent residents—definitely a bird-watcher's dream. More than 50 mammals of both land and sea live here, too. Harbor seals occasionally use the tip of the spit as a pup-raising site. In the bay, eelgrass beds provide a nursery for young salmon and steelhead adjusting to saltwater. This is a wonderful place to enjoy the wildlife.

Directions

From Seattle, drive north on I-5 to Exit 177, signed Highway 104 and Edmonds/Kingston Ferry. Drive west on Highway 104 to the Edmonds/Kingston Ferry Terminal and ride the ferry to Kingston (a 30-minute trip). From Kingston, drive west on Highway 104 across the Hood Canal Bridge to U.S. Highway 101. Turn north on U.S. 101, go just west of Sequim, and turn north on Kitchen-Dick Road. Continue for three miles to the Dungeness Recreation Area. Go through the recreation area to the refuge parking lot at the end of the road. The well-marked trailhead is located immediately before the parking area.

Information and Contact

Most of this area is accessible year-round (some parts are closed seasonally to protect wildlife feeding and nesting). This trail is open to hikers only—dogs are strictly prohibited. The entrance fee is $3 per family daily. Admission is free with a federal duck stamp, a Golden Eagle Pass, a Golden Age Pass, or a Golden Access passport. For a topographic map, ask the USGS for Dungeness. For more information, contact Dungeness National Wildlife Refuge, Washington Maritime NWR Complex, 33 South Barr Road, Port Angeles, WA 98362, 360/457-8451.

② MOUNT ZION
Olympic National Forest

Level: Easy/Moderate

Total Distance: 3.6 miles

Hiking Time: 2 hours

Elevation Gain: 1,300 feet

Summary: A short climb to views of the Olympic interior and Puget Sound atop Mount Zion.

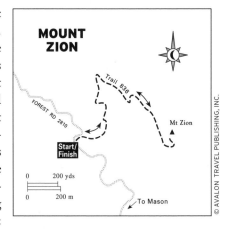

Mount Zion is one of the Olympic Mountains' most accessible peaks. Standing apart from the rest of the range, the mountain offers great views of Puget Sound laid out before Mount Baker and the Cascades. The forested trail gains a modest 1,300 feet in just under two miles. The trail's best attraction is the many rhododendrons that grace the forest along the entire route. They are in full bloom during June and are likely to be a lasting memory of the hike. An added bonus: the mountain is located in the Olympics' rain shadow. Rainy days in Seattle may not be as wet on Mount Zion.

A quick disclaimer: Reaching the trailhead from Seattle takes longer than two hours, depending on your wait for the ferry. The trailhead is about an hour and 15 minutes from Kingston, the western ferry terminal. Just remember that time moves slowly on the peninsula—clock watchers are quickly chastised. This relatively short and easy day hike is a great part of a day spent sightseeing on the peninsula.

Mount Zion Trail is a straightforward hike. It's one trail all the way to the summit. There are no junctions or confusing footpaths leading off into the forest. The tread is wide, flat, and in excellent condition. The grade is a steady incline but is never steep. Kids as young as six years old should be able to reach the summit with encouragement. Keep them close on trail, however, as several sections of trail traverse a hillside that has steep drop-offs.

From the trailhead, Mount Zion Trail enters the forest and begins climbing toward the summit. The route turns north (0.3 mile) to make one long switchback up the hillside. The second-growth forest is cool and shady.

Rhododendrons, salal, and huckleberry bushes fill the understory. The trail's only view until the summit is a good one through an opening in the forest (1.5 miles). A full spread of Mount Townsend, Iron and Buckhorn Mountains, and The Needles is revealed to the southwest. This is a good reason to bring a map. A final push reaches the summit of Mount Zion (1.8 miles). Trees are encroaching on the views, but there is still much to see, with Puget Sound, Mount Baker, and other Cascade peaks lining the western horizon.

Directions
From Seattle, drive north on I-5 to Exit 177, signed Highway 104 and Edmonds/Kingston Ferry. Drive west on Highway 104 to the Edmonds/Kingston Ferry Terminal and ride the ferry to Kingston (a 30-minute trip). From Kingston, drive west on Highway 104 across the Hood Canal Bridge to U.S. Highway 101. Turn south on U.S. 101 and drive eight miles to Lords Lake Loop. Turn right and drive three miles to Lords Lake—stay to the left at the lake. At four miles, cross the forest boundary; the road becomes Forest Service Road 28. At eight miles, turn right at a four-way junction and continue on Forest Service Road 28. At nine miles, turn right on Forest Service Road 2810. At 11 miles, Mount Zion trailhead is on the right and parking is on the left.

Information and Contact
This trail is accessible mid-May–November (year-round with snowshoes) and is open to hikers and leashed dogs. A federal Northwest Forest Pass is required to park here. For a map of Olympic National Forest, contact the Outdoor Recreation Information Center at the downtown Seattle REI. For topographic maps, ask Green Trails for No. 136, Tyler Peak, or ask the USGS for Mount Zion. For more information, contact Olympic National Forest, Quilcene Ranger Station, 295142 U.S. 101 South, Quilcene, WA 98376, 360/765-2200.

3 MOUNT TOWNSEND   BEST ☾

in the Buckhorn Wilderness of Olympic National Forest

🏕 🚴 🌲 🐕 🚶

Level: Moderate   **Total Distance:** 7.8 miles

Hiking Time: 5 hours   **Elevation Gain:** 3,400 feet

Summary: A beautiful but challenging ascent to the summit of Mount Townsend and some of the peninsula's best views.

Upon reaching the summit of Mount Townsend, hikers may be hard pressed to decide if they're in the midst of mountains or perched above long stretches of Puget waterways. This lofty summit strategically puts you smack dab in the middle of the two settings. The grand, competing vistas are likely to vie for your attention for the length of your stay here. Be

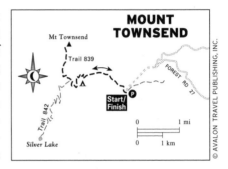

thankful. High mountain meadows scrubbed by forceful winds, complete with requisite berries, complement the experience. It's no wonder that Mount Townsend is one of the peninsula's more popular day hikes.

Before you hit the road, be aware that reaching the trailhead from Seattle takes longer than two hours, depending on your wait for the ferry. The trailhead is about one hour and 15 minutes from Kingston, the western ferry terminal. Still, this is a very popular day hike for people coming from the east side of Puget Sound.

With 3,400 feet of elevation gain, the trek up Mount Townsend is no easy endeavor. Be prepared for a long hike and, on sunny days, a hot hike. Extra water and sunscreen are a hiker's best friends during the summer. Surprisingly, the summit can be a chilly experience. The top of Mount Townsend is barren and extremely windy. Despite the heat, a warm layer will be well cherished at the mountain's summit.

Mount Townsend Trail climbs steadily throughout its length. The first two miles pass through forest punctuated by rhododendrons (catch them blooming in early summer). Eventually the timber thins, and views of Puget Sound accompany hikers. At 2.5 miles lies Camp Windy (not nearly as windy as Townsend's summit) and a pair of small ponds. Just beyond camp, Mount Townsend Trail reaches a signed junction with Silver Lakes Trail (2.9 miles).

Mount Townsend Trail turns right and harshly climbs through open meadows of juniper and huckleberry bushes. Snow and wind limit the growth of the subalpine trees, leaving vistas for hikers. This steep section of trail is the hike's most challenging and most scenic section. The trail reaches the long, barren summit of Mount Townsend in a sea of views (3.9 miles). To the east, the North Cascades are spread out behind Puget Sound, while Mount Deception and The Needles are highlights of the Olympic Range. Mount Townsend Trail continues down the north side of Mount Townsend, but hikers should turn around and descend by retracing the route.

Directions

From Seattle, drive north on I-5 to Exit 177, signed Highway 104 and Edmonds/Kingston Ferry. Drive west on Highway 104 to the Edmonds/Kingston Ferry Terminal and ride the ferry to Kingston (a 30-minute trip). From Kingston, drive west on Highway 104 across the Hood Canal Bridge. Ten miles after the bridge, turn right at the cutoff for Quilcene (Center Road). Turn right on Center Road and drive 10 miles to U.S. 101 in Quilcene.

From Quilcene, drive one mile south on U.S. 101 to Penny Creek Road. Turn right and drive 1.5 miles to Big Quilcene Road. Stay left at this Y and drive three miles to the Forest Service boundary, where the dirt road becomes paved Forest Service Road 27. At 6.5 miles, pass Forest Service Road 2750 and stay to the right. At 9.5 miles, pass Forest Service Road 2760 (signed Mount Townsend Trail 1 mile) and again stay to the right. At 11 miles, turn left on an unnumbered road (also signed Mount Townsend Trail 1 mile). Drive one mile to the signed trailhead at road's end.

Information and Contact

This trail is accessible June–October (year-round with snowshoes) and is open to hikers and leashed dogs. A federal Northwest Forest Pass is required to park here. For a map of Olympic National Forest, contact the Outdoor Recreation Information Center at the downtown Seattle REI. For topographic maps, ask Green Trails for No. 136, Tyler Peak, or ask the USGS for Mount Townsend. For more information, contact Olympic National Forest, Quilcene Ranger Station, 295142 U.S. 101 South, Quilcene, WA 98376, 360/765-2200.

4 SILVER LAKE

in the Buckhorn Wilderness of Olympic National Forest

Level: Moderate/Strenuous   **Total Distance:** 10.8 miles

Hiking Time: 7 hours   **Elevation Gain:** 3,500 feet

Summary: A scenic but challenging hike to a remote Olympic beauty.

A trip to Silver Lake is a full day. First, the trip to the trail is about two hours, with the ferry ride. Second, the hike itself is nearly 11 miles with plenty of elevation change. Nonetheless, this is a manageable day hike. In fact, it's one of the Olympics' best destinations, thus its inclusion here. Within a large basin rimmed with jagged peaks, Silver Lake and subalpine firs mingle with meadows of heather. There are actually two Silver Lakes, but this trip visits only the larger and more scenic of the pair.

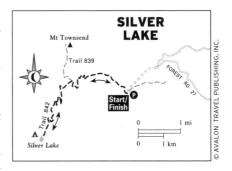

The hike to Silver Lakes begins on Mount Townsend Trail. The route soon enters Buckhorn Wilderness (0.3 mile) and climbs steadily through the forest. Rhododendrons are prolific in this rain-shadow forest. Eventually the timber thins to reveal views of Puget Sound. At 2.5 miles lies Camp Windy and a pair of small ponds. Just beyond this camp, the trail reaches the junction with Silver Lakes Trail (2.9 miles). This section of trail is a respectable ascent, gaining 2,500 feet in under three miles—nothing to shake your head at. Plenty of water and trail snacks will be much appreciated.

It's also a good idea to bring a map on this hike. Beyond the junction, the trail feels wild and is not heavily traveled. Head east on Silver Lakes Trail as it reaches the ridgeline and quickly descends into Silver Creek Valley. The trail drops 500 feet from the junction to a crossing of Silver Creek (4.5 miles) and then climbs 400 feet to the larger and more popular of the Silver Lakes (5.4 miles). The smaller lake is due north and accessed by unofficial and obscure footpaths—it's not a recommended side trip. The upper Silver Lake has quite enough to offer.

Upper Silver Lake is one of the Olympics' most scenic lakes. Parkland surrounds the lake, with large meadows of wildflowers mingling with small stands of subalpine fir. Stocked with trout, the lake is a prime backcountry fishing hole. Rocky ridges nearly surround the basin. If you have the energy left, be sure to scramble the slope rising to the south, between rocky peaks, for more wildflowers and prime views of the Olympic Range. If you wish to turn this long day hike into an overnight backpacking trip, there are several campsites at the lake.

Directions

From Seattle, drive north on I-5 to Exit 177, signed Highway 104 and Edmonds/Kingston Ferry. Drive west on Highway 104 to the Edmonds/Kingston Ferry Terminal and ride the ferry to Kingston (a 30-minute trip). From Kingston, drive west on Highway 104 across the Hood Canal Bridge. Ten miles after the bridge, turn right at the cutoff for Quilcene (Center Road). Turn right on Center Road and drive 10 miles to U.S. 101 in Quilcene.

From Quilcene, drive one mile south on U.S. 101 to Penny Creek Road. Turn right and drive 1.5 miles to Big Quilcene Road. Stay left at this Y and drive three miles to the Forest Service boundary, where the dirt road becomes paved Forest Service Road 27. At 6.5 miles, pass Forest Service Road 2750 and stay to the right. At 9.5 miles, pass Forest Service Road 2760 (signed Mount Townsend Trail 1 mile) and again stay to the right. At 11 miles, turn left on an unnumbered road (also signed Mount Townsend Trail 1 mile). Drive one mile to the signed trailhead at road's end.

Information and Contact

This trail is accessible July–October and is open to hikers and leashed dogs. A federal Northwest Forest Pass is required to park here. For a map of Olympic National Forest, contact the Outdoor Recreation Information Center at the downtown Seattle REI. For topographic maps, ask Green Trails for No. 136, Tyler Peak, or ask the USGS for Mount Townsend. For more information, contact Olympic National Forest, Quilcene Ranger Station, 295142 U.S. 101 South, Quilcene, WA 98376, 360/765-2200.

5 UPPER BIG QUILCENE TRAIL

in the Buckhorn Wilderness of Olympic National Forest

Level: Moderate/Strenuous   **Total Distance:** 10.6 miles

Hiking Time: 6 hours   **Elevation Gain:** 3,700 feet

Summary: One of the Olympic Mountains' best day hikes, from old-growth forest to amazing views at meadowy Marmot Pass.

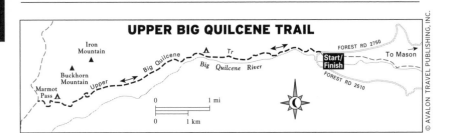

Rarely can hikers get to such an outstanding viewpoint, with so much wild country spread before them, than with Upper Big Quilcene Trail. Passing through virgin timber and open, flowery meadows, this hike reaches heaven at Marmot Pass. This is an opportunity to view many of the Olympics' most impressive peaks, including Mount Mystery and Mount Deception. The trail is one of the best on the peninsula's east side and perfect for an outing with the dog.

Getting out to this trailhead is rarely quick and easy. Be aware that the drive from Seattle takes a little longer than two hours, depending on your wait for the ferry. The trailhead is about an hour and 20 minutes from Kingston, the western ferry terminal. Still, this is a very popular day hike for people coming from the east side of Puget Sound.

The trail gains a considerable amount of elevation (3,700 feet), but it is spread evenly throughout the route. The last half mile is the most challenging. From the trailhead, Upper Big Quilcene Trail quickly enters the Buckhorn Wilderness and ascends steadily. The trail parallels the Big Quilcene River for several miles, where the forest consists of old-growth Douglas fir, western hemlock, and western red cedar. In June, rhododendrons light up the understory with fragrant blossoms. The trail reaches Shelter Rock Camp at the perfect time for a break (2.6 miles).

Located on the Olympics' leeward side, the Big Quilcene Valley lies in the rain shadow of the mountain range. This region receives much less rain than the western Olympics or western Cascades and is a good day-hiking alternative when the forecast is less than great for western Washington. From Shelter Rock, Upper Big Quilcene Trail continues climbing through forest and slopes of talus. The trail encounters Camp Mystery beside a small stream (4.6 miles) before making the final climb to Marmot Pass (5.3 miles). The pass is awash in meadows. Marmots will likely greet you with a whistle. This is one of the Olympic Mountains' best views. Lining the western horizon are some of the range's tallest peaks, including Mount Mystery, Mount Deception, and The Needles. To the south are the craggy summits of Warrior Peak and Mount Constance.

Options
This hike works very well as an overnight backpacking trip. A pair of good camps are located on the trail. Shelter Rock (2.6 miles) and Camp Mystery (4.6 miles) have several sites each and are both next to water. No permits are needed to camp.

Directions
From Seattle, drive north on I-5 to Exit 177, signed Highway 104 and Edmonds/Kingston Ferry. Drive west on Highway 104 to the Edmonds/Kingston Ferry Terminal and ride the ferry to Kingston (a 30-minute trip). From Kingston, drive west on Highway 104 across the Hood Canal Bridge. Ten miles after the bridge, turn right at the cutoff for Quilcene (Center Road). Turn right on Center Road and drive 10 miles to U.S. 101 in Quilcene.

From Quilcene, drive one mile south on U.S. 101 to Penny Creek Road. Turn right and drive 1.5 miles to Big Quilcene Road. Stay left at this Y and drive three miles to the Forest Service boundary, where the dirt road becomes paved Forest Service Road 27. Continue on Forest Service Road 27 and drive 6.5 miles to Forest Service Road 2750. Stay to the left at this Y and drive five miles to the signed trailhead on the right with parking on the left.

Information and Contact
This trail is accessible mid-June–October and is open to hikers and leashed dogs. A federal Northwest Forest Pass is required to park here. For a map of Olympic National Forest, contact the Outdoor Recreation Information Center at the downtown Seattle REI. For topographic maps, ask Green Trails for No. 136, Tyler Peak, or ask the USGS for Mount Townsend and Mount Deception. For more information, contact Olympic National Forest, Quilcene Ranger Station, 295142 U.S. 101 South, Quilcene, WA 98376, 360/765-2200.

MOUNTAIN LOOP HIGHWAY

© SCOTT LEONARD

BEST HIKES

The Mountain Loop Highway offers access to many incredible mountains and peaks that rise straight up from the river valleys on some of the Cascade's most difficult but most scenic day hikes. From Darrington, the highway delves into the mountains to Barlow Pass before coming out of the mountains to Granite Falls. Although designated a National Scenic Byway, portions of this route are nothing more than a well-maintained gravel road.

Darrington, the northern access point of the highway, is home to a pair of great river hikes: Boulder River features great old-growth forest, spectacular waterfalls, and a quiet hike in the off-season, and the Old Sauk Trail follows the river through a forest of big trees where you can spot bald eagles and salmon on their spawning runs. The northern half of the Mountain Loop Highway has a few big peaks, as well. Mount Higgins and Mount Pugh are great summit hikes offering incredible views.

The apex of the highway, at Barlow Pass, provides access to the old mining town of Monte Cristo. Here, an old road has been closed to motorized traffic and is now accessed by bike or foot to three challenging hikes. Gothic Basin, Glacier Basin, and Poodle Dog Pass are steep hikes to incredible views beneath towering mountains. If the challenge of scaling these big trails sounds like too much, the easy and gentle hike to historic Monte Cristo is recommended. Remnants of the old town still exist, including numerous historical artifacts.

The southern arm of the Mountain Loop Highway features subalpine meadows, lakes, and enjoyable family hikes. Mount Forgotten Meadows, Mount Dickerman, and Goat Flats are sublime hikes to expansive views and huckleberry meadows. Lake 22 and Heather Lake lie beneath the towering granite walls of Mount Pilchuck and feature trails that ring each lake. Cutthroat Lakes is a little-known trail that visits a string of outstanding lakes surrounded by meadows.

Due to record rainfall in October 2003, a segment of the highway at its most eastern stretch has been washed out. The road from southern Bedal Creek to Barlow Pass is currently inaccessible to vehicles, but is still open to bicyclists and hikers. Construction on this historic portion of the route has already begun and the road is scheduled to reopen in Fall 2006. The only trail affected by the closure is Goat Lake, now a longer but still accessible hike.

Exploring this highly recommended region is a scenic endeavor and offers adventure for hikers of all abilities. Although many of the hikes in this chapter are moderate to strenuous in terms of difficulty, some are perfect for an easy, family outing. Big Four Ice Caves is an outstanding natural phenomenon in the spring, when melting snow creates large caves in a snowfield. Ashland Lakes is an easy hike to four different lakes and a large waterfall, and Heather Lake and Mount Pilchuck are good for older children.

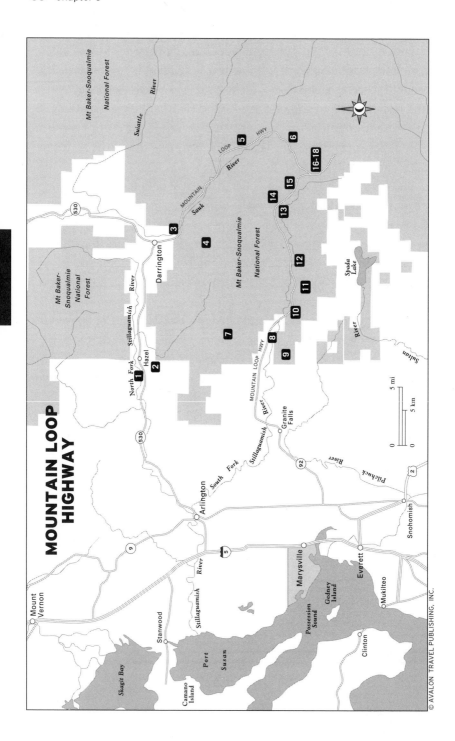

MOUNTAIN LOOP HIGHWAY

Mt Baker-Snoqualmie National Forest

Suiattle River

Mt Baker-Snoqualmie National Forest

LOOP HWY

MOUNTAIN

Sauk River

Darrington

Mt Baker-Snoqualmie National Forest

Spada Lake

River

Sultan

Stillaguamish River

North Fork

Hazel

MOUNTAIN LOOP HWY

Stillaguamish River

Granite Falls

South Fork

Stillaguamish

Arlington

Pilchuck River

Snohomish

Stillaguamish River

Stanwood

Marysville

Possession Sound

Gedney Island

Everett

Mukilteo

Clinton

Mount Vernon

Skagit Bay

Camano Island

Port Susan

5 mi

5 km

© AVALON TRAVEL PUBLISHING, INC.

Mountain Loop Highway Hikes

■1 MOUNT HIGGINS

Mount Baker-Snoqualmie National Forest

🏠 🐕 🏃

Level: Strenuous   **Total Distance:** 9 miles

Hiking Time: 6 hours   **Elevation Gain:** 3,400 feet

Summary: A strenuous climb to an outstanding viewpoint of Puget Sound and the Cascades.

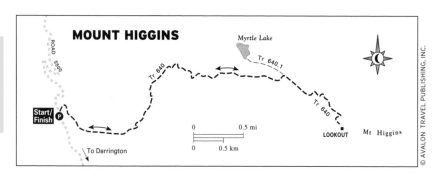

Mount Higgins is best known by Mountain Loop Highway drivers as the first big mountain they pass under. Highly visible from the road is the long band of rock capping the ridge and leading into the tilted slats of Mount Higgins. The hike up is every bit as rewarding and as strenuous as it would seem from the car. On the western edge of the Cascades, the peak is the former site of a forest service lookout and offers expansive views in every direction.

Make no mistake, a trek to the summit of Mount Higgins is a trip for serious hikers. Mount Higgins Trail endures 3,400 feet of harsh elevation gain on the way—that's a lot of climbing. Sections of the trail are muddy and boggy, and the bugs are notoriously bad during the early summer. Be prepared to grind it out to savor the views at the end.

Mount Higgins Trail begins on land managed by the state Department of Natural Resources. After passing through a shady stretch of forest, the trail enters typical DNR land—a large clear-cut (0.5 mile). The ascent is steep and sometimes rocky as it crosses the Forest Service boundary (1.2 miles). Many of the wooden structures along the route are rotten and unstable. Fortunately, the stream crossings are small and manageable without the bridges.

The trail begins to level out as it enters a marshy area and an unsigned junction (3.3 miles). A left turn drops to Myrtle Lake, a buggy forested lake. The lake, although popular with anglers, is not worth the time. Turn right and remain on Mount Higgins Trail as it continues climbing. The final, steep ascent switchbacks through forest and rock fields to the journey's end atop Mount Higgins' western peak (4.5 miles). It's a sheer 4,500 drop to the Stillaguamish Valley from the decrepit remains of an old fire lookout. To the north, east, and south are outstanding views of countless Cascade peaks. Puget Sound and the Olympics lie to the west.

Directions

From Seattle, drive north on I-5 to Exit 208, Highway 530 to Arlington and Darrington. Turn right and drive east on Highway 530, through Arlington (four miles). From Arlington, drive 18 miles to a gravel road on the left, signed C-Post Road (just before milepost 38). Turn left and drive four miles (across the Stillaguamish River) to the signed trailhead at road's end.

Information and Contact

This trail is accessible June–October and is open to hikers and leashed dogs. A federal Northwest Forest Pass is required to park here. For a map of Mount Baker–Snoqualmie National Forest, contact the Outdoor Recreation Information Center at the downtown Seattle REI. For topographic maps, ask Green Trails for No. 77, Oso, or ask the USGS for Mount Higgins. For more information, contact Mount Baker–Snoqualmie National Forest, Darrington Ranger Station, 1405 Emmens Street, Darrington, WA 98241, 360/436-1155.

2 BOULDER RIVER   BEST [

in the Boulder River Wilderness of Mount Baker-Snoqualmie
National Forest

Level: Easy   **Total Distance:** 8.6 miles

Hiking Time: 4.5 hours   **Elevation Gain:** 650 feet

Summary: A laid-back stroll along the Boulder River with big trees and big
waterfalls along the way.

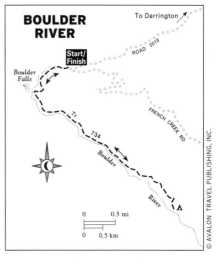

Some days just aren't made for the high country. The Cascades' wet and heavy snowfall puts the higher elevations out of reach in winter and spring. And it's not unheard of for it to be raining cats and dogs (cougars and bears, in wilderness speak) in the middle of July. Boulder River Trail is an excellent alternative to the high country in these times of foul weather, offering hikers a chance to stretch the legs and get ready for summer. The trail wanders more than four miles into this wild river valley to a picturesque setting on the river.

Along the way are several outstanding waterfalls dropping into the river, which makes much of its way through narrow gorges. With little elevation gain, the trail is a favorite for hikers of all ages and abilities.

Rain or shine all year-round, Boulder River is open for business. Substantial snowfall at this low elevation is uncommon—the valley rarely sees anything more than a dusting of snow. Thus, this is a great choice for an outing from the fall through the spring. And on cloudy days, who cares if the sun doesn't shine when you're immersed amongst the forest's big trees. Naturally, this is a popular trail—don't be surprised to find the local scout troop camped at trail's end.

Boulder River Trail begins by gently climbing along an old logging road. Down to the right are peek-a-boo views of Boulder Falls (0.4 mile). The trail reaches a crest and soon crosses the wilderness boundary (0.8 mile), where great old-growth forest begins. The journey's biggest waterfall soon comes into view, where it plunges down a cliff into the river (1.3 miles). Spring

© SCOTT LEONARD

The hiking is best in the Boulder River Wilderness during spring or fall.

snowmelt makes this a dandy of a cascade—another reason this route offers good early-season hiking. This is a nice picnic or resting spot, with a beach on the trail side of the river across from the waterfall.

Boulder River Trail continues through exceptional old-growth forests. Early-season hikers will encounter numerous trilliums and other understory flowers in full bloom. Sometimes the trail climbs above the noisy river, which runs intermittently through narrow canyons. The trail can be muddy and riddled with roots in places, evidence of the valley's wet temperament.

Boulder River Trail reaches its end when it empties out onto the river's banks (4.3 miles). Three Fingers Peak can be seen up the valley. Expect to linger here a while, poking around the brush for nice, sandy beaches. Boulder River is a great overnight trip as well, with several campsites clustered around the end of the trail.

Directions

From Seattle, drive north on I-5 to Exit 208, Arlington/Darrington. Turn right and drive east on Highway 530 through Arlington (four miles). Continue on Mountain Loop Highway (Highway 530) 19 miles to French Creek Road. Turn right and drive four miles to the signed trailhead at road's end.

Information and Contact

This trail is accessible year-round and is open to hikers and leashed dogs. A federal Northwest Forest Pass is required to park here. For a map of Mount Baker–Snoqualmie National Forest, contact the Outdoor Recreation Information Center at the downtown Seattle REI. For topographic maps, ask Green Trails for No. 77, Oso, and No. 109, Granite Falls, or ask the USGS for Mount Higgins and Meadow Mountain. For more information, contact Mount Baker–Snoqualmie National Forest, Darrington Ranger Station, 1405 Emmens Street, Darrington, WA 98241, 360/436-1155.

3 OLD SAUK TRAIL

Mount Baker-Snoqualmie National Forest

Level: Easy

Total Distance: 6.0 miles

Hiking Time: 3 hours

Elevation Gain: 100 feet

Summary: An easy stroll through lush green forests along the banks of the Sauk River.

Old Sauk is a pleasant exception to the typical hike of the Mountain Loop Highway. In stark contrast to the rugged climbs and big views of many hikes in this area, Old Sauk Trail is an easy ramble along the milky gray waters of the Sauk River. This is a great hike for families with young kids—the trail is level with no shortage of things to see. Wildlife can be found in the rumbling waters of the Sauk, on land in the lush forest, and in the air along this hike. A hike in any season is a peaceful experience. Rarely are easy hikes so memorable.

Old Sauk Trail is three miles in length one-way. From the trailhead at the signed parking area, it enters the forest and parallels the river for its entirety. Much of the forest along the trail was logged in the early 20th century. It has since regrown into a mossy, lush forest. There are several stream crossings but each is bridged. In October 2003, intense rainfall flooded the river and wiped out several sections of Old Sauk Trail, not to mention dozens of other trails and roads in the area. Fortunately, the Forest Service and volunteer crews quickly repaired damaged tread and rerouted small segments. The trail is once again in good shape.

The opportunities for viewing wildlife are great. Elk and deer are frequent grazers in the forest. In the small streams crossing the river, you can see small salmon darting under woody debris. Be sure to stay out of the streams, though—this is a fragile home to the endangered fish. Eagles and ospreys are commonly seen cruising from perch to perch beside the river. Best of all, Old Sauk is a hike for any season. Winter brings little more than dustings of snow. Early summer is berry season, when salmonberries, huckleberries, and thimbleberries are the culprits of stained fingers. And in the fall, salmon return to the Sauk to spawn.

Directions

From Seattle, drive north on I-5 to Exit 208, Highway 530 to Arlington and Darrington. Turn right and drive east on Highway 530, through Arlington (four miles), to the town of Darrington (31 miles). At the stop sign in the center of town, turn right on Mountain Loop Highway and drive four miles to the signed parking area and trailhead on the left.

Information and Contact

This trail is accessible year-round and is open to hikers and leashed dogs. A federal Northwest Forest Pass is required to park here. For a map of

Stands of old growth line the banks of the Sauk River.

Mount Baker–Snoqualmie National Forest, contact the Outdoor Recreation Information Center at the downtown Seattle REI. For topographic maps, ask Green Trails for No. 110, Silverton, or ask the USGS for Helena Ridge. For more information, contact Mount Baker–Snoqualmie National Forest, Darrington Ranger Station, 1405 Emmens Street, Darrington, WA 98241, 360/436-1155.

4 SQUIRE CREEK PASS

Mount Baker-Snoqualmie National Forest

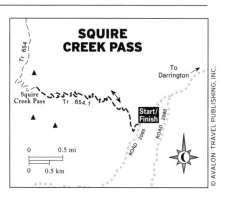

Level: Moderate/Strenuous **Total Distance:** 5.0 miles

Hiking Time: 4 hours **Elevation Gain:** 2,300 feet

Summary: This is an alternate route to scenic Squire Creek Pass.

This hike is an alternative to the traditional route to Squire Creek Pass, once a popular destination in the Boulder River Wilderness. The pass was previously accessed by Squire Creek Trail—that is, until a large washout on the road made it dangerous and ill-advised for travel. Fortunately there are two trails to Squire Creek Pass. Eight-Mile Creek Trail is the alternative route and approaches the pass from the east. Hiking Eight-Mile Creek is not as grand or scenic as the old route, but Squire Creek Pass is as scenic as ever. Recent work on Eight-Mile Creek Trail has ensured that Squire Creek Pass remains a good day hike.

With so much storm damage to key roads in the area, the road to the old trailhead is low on the priority list. So the Forest Service has invested in this alternative route by maintaining it. What was once a rugged and neglected path with lots of blown-down trees is now a much easier to follow trail. Maintenance does not change the nature of the hike, however, which is up, up, and up—2,300 feet in 2.5 miles is a hearty climb.

Hiking Eight-Mile Creek Trail is straightforward and simple—it leaves the road and sharply climbs to Squire Creek Pass (2.5 miles). Much of the route is shrouded in dense forest, so the views wait until the end. At one mile, the trail passes beneath Three O' Clock Rock, a popular rock-climbing site. The trail crosses numerous small streams as they cascade down the steep hillside. The forest begins to thin into a subalpine mix and passes several small tarns (2.1 miles). The trail reaches pay dirt at Squire Creek Pass (2.5 miles), where the views open up and reveal the heart of the Boulder River Wilderness: Three Fingers and Whitehorse Mountain. Mountain goats are becoming an increasingly rare sighting on the surrounding ridges, but lucky hikers will spot one of

the view of Whitehorse Mountain from Squire Creek Pass

the furry creatures. Huckleberries are prolific in August and from June–July many interesting bugs can be spotted along the trail.

Directions

From Seattle, drive north on I-5 to Exit 208, Highway 530 to Arlington and Darrington. Turn right and drive east on Highway 530, through Arlington (four miles), to the town of Darrington (31 miles). At the stop sign in the center of town, turn right on Mountain Loop Highway and drive three miles to Forest Service Road 2060, across from Clear Creek Campground. Turn right and drive six miles to the road's only fork. Stay to the right, now on Road 2065, and drive 0.5 mile to the signed trailhead on the right.

Information and Contact

This trail is accessible mid-June–October and is open to hikers and leashed dogs. A federal Northwest Forest Pass is required to park here. For a map of Mount Baker–Snoqualmie National Forest, contact the Outdoor Recreation Information Center at the downtown Seattle REI. For topographic maps, ask Green Trails for No. 110, Silverton, or ask the USGS for Helena Ridge and Whitehorse Mountain. For more information, contact Mount Baker–Snoqualmie National Forest, Darrington Ranger Station, 1405 Emmens Street, Darrington, WA 98241, 360/436-1155.

5 STUJACK PASS

BEST ◖

Mount Baker-Snoqualmie National Forest

Level: Strenuous

Total Distance: 8.0 miles

Hiking Time: 7 hours

Elevation Gain: 3,900 feet

Summary: A punishing ascent through shady forest to meadows and big mountain views with an even more difficult option to the summit of Mount Pugh.

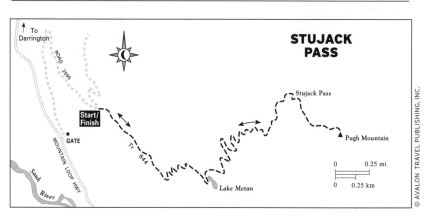

In true North Cascades form, Mount Pugh Trail makes a challenging climb (nearly 4,000 feet) to expansive views that encompass a multitude of peaks. Stujack Pass is a small saddle on the ridge below mighty Pugh Mountain. The terrain is inspiring, with patches of small, weather-beaten trees growing in gardens of rock and heather. If this isn't enough, there is a footpath that leads to the summit of Mount Pugh. The question won't be if you want to summit Mount Pugh. The question will be if you have the energy to summit Mount Pugh.

The trip to Stujack Pass is unarguably a difficult hike. The continuously steep grade is strenuous not only on the way up but also on the way down. Be stocked with plenty of water and trail snacks for the trip, especially on hot summer days. Although Stujack Pass is just eight miles round-trip, the elevation gain makes it feel like much more. It's a great hike, but just be aware of what lies ahead.

Mount Pugh Trail traverses the hillside and crosses several small streams while steadily gaining elevation. The first of many switchbacks signals the start of the climb in earnest (0.9 mile). Soon the trail enters old-growth forest and encounters small Lake Metan (1.7 miles). Lacking views but not bugs, Lake Metan is a less-than-spectacular break point.

© PATTI BLEIFUSS

The hike to Stujack Pass is one of the steepest and most challenging day hikes.

The harshest but most beautiful part of the hike is just ahead as Mount Pugh Trail climbs the steep hillside. As the forest thins (3.2 miles), the spoils of the hike are revealed in the form of big views to the east. The tread is sometimes rocky but always in good shape to the pass. A very sharp climb of talus fields abruptly achieves the welcome sight of Stujack Pass (4.0 miles). The pass is a small gap in the ridge of Pugh Mountain—the hillsides are a canvas of color from blooming wildflowers in July. The views, from Rainier to Baker, embrace too much of the Cascades to absorb in just one afternoon.

Options

Hearty and experienced hikers with a wealth of energy will enjoy the challenge of summiting Mount Pugh. A summit trip adds 1.2 miles and a daunting 1,500 feet of elevation. From Stujack Pass, a narrow footpath heads south along the ridge. The ascent is steep, and many sections are rock scrambles. The climb is not technical, but a couple segments drop sharply and are sure to get the adrenaline running. Enjoy the views and be careful.

Directions

From Seattle, drive north on I-5 to Exit 208, Highway 530 to Arlington and Darrington. Turn right and drive east on Highway 530, through Arlington (four miles), to the town of Darrington (31 miles). At the stop sign in the center of town, turn right on Mountain Loop Highway and drive 13 miles to discreetly signed Forest Service Road 2095. Turn left and drive two miles to the signed trailhead above a sharp switchback in the road.

Information and Contact

This trail is accessible August–October and is open to hikers and leashed dogs. A federal Northwest Forest Pass is required to park here. For a map of Mount Baker–Snoqualmie National Forest, contact the Outdoor Recreation Information Center at the downtown Seattle REI. For topographic maps, ask Green Trails for No. 111, Sloan Peak, or ask the USGS for White Chuck Mountain. For more information, contact Mount Baker–Snoqualmie National Forest, Darrington Ranger Station, 1405 Emmens Street, Darrington, WA 98241, 360/436-1155.

6 GOAT LAKE

in the Henry M. Jackson Wilderness of Mount Baker-Snoqualmie National Forest

Level: Easy/Moderate

Total Distance: 9.4-15.4 miles

Hiking Time: 5-8 hours

Elevation Gain: 1,300 feet

Summary: This Mountain Loop Highway favorite is an easy hike to a grand lake in a dramatic setting.

Goat Lake has traditionally been one of the most popular hikes on the Mountain Loop Highway. Of course, an easy hike through old-growth forest to waterfalls and a scenic lake is always going to have a good reputation. For the last few years, however, reaching Goat Lake has been more difficult. A record storm in October 2003 washed out a portion of the Mountain Loop Highway near the hike's trailhead, adding six round-trip miles to the hike. Repairs are slated to be completed by fall 2006, but be sure to call the Verlot Public Service Center for the most current information. The washout makes Goat Lake a long trip but it is certainly still worth it. The opportunity to see wildlife along the way is first-rate right now because of the seclusion of the area.

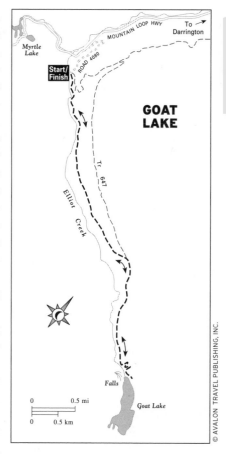

To access Goat Lake while the Mountain Loop Highway is still washed out, follow the normal driving directions to the road closure just past Barlow Pass. Park here and walk or bike along the graveled Mountain Loop Highway to Forest Road 4080. Take a right and hike one mile to the traditional trailhead for Elliot Creek Trail.

From the established trailhead, there are actually two routes to Goat Lake.

The first route utilizes an old road-bed which once serviced the mining community at the lake. This route has a more steady elevation gain but is not as scenic. The recommended route, detailed here, wanders up the valley beside the noisy creek in a grand forest. The two trails merge 1.6 miles before Goat Lake and share the same trail to the lake. This is a good hike for families—a little long but without a lot of elevation gain.

Elliot Creek Trail starts at the far right side of the parking lot at the trailhead and quickly finds Elliot Creek, nearly big enough to be called a river. The grade is gentle and gains just 700 feet in the first three miles. The tread is well maintained and does its best to keep feet dry. This is a great section of forest, where

winter snow on Foggy Peak at the backside of Goat Lake

patches of ferns and moss fill in between big firs and cedars. Eventually the old forest gives way to second-growth, and the trail makes its first stream crossing (2.8 miles). The trail junctions with the logging road trail (3.1 miles)—continue hiking up the valley.

The trail crosses three more small streams, the second being the wilderness boundary (4.0 miles), and comes to the only section of notable elevation gain. A series of switchbacks climbs up beside noisy McIntosh Falls on Elliot Creek (4.4 miles). The falls are mostly hidden from the trail, but their roar is unmistakable. The trail then reaches the north end of Goat Lake (4.7 miles) and the splendor of the large basin. Indomitable Foggy Peak towers over the lake, which is ringed by meadows and subalpine forest.

Directions

From Seattle, drive north on I-90 to Everett and turn east on Highway 2. Drive two miles and turn east on Highway 204 to Lake Stevens. Drive three miles and turn north on Highway 9 to Lake Stevens. Drive two miles and turn east on Highway 92. Drive nine miles straight through the town of Granite Falls. At the end of town, turn left on the Mountain Loop Highway (signed to Verlot and Darrington). Drive 30 miles east on the Mountain Loop Highway, through the towns of Verlot and Silverton, to Barlow Pass, where the pavement ends and the gravel begins. Continue driving on Mountain Loop Highway, now toward Darrington, four miles to Forest Service Road 4080. Turn right and drive one mile to the trailhead at road's end.

Information and Contact

This trail is accessible June–October and is open to hikers and leashed dogs. A federal Northwest Forest Pass is required to park here. For a map of Mount Baker–Snoqualmie National Forest, contact the Outdoor Recreation Information Center at the downtown Seattle REI. For topographic maps, ask Green Trails for No. 111, Sloan Peak, or ask the USGS for Bedal and Sloan Peak. For more information, contact Mount Baker–Snoqualmie National Forest, Verlot Public Service Center, 33515 Mountain Loop Highway, Granite Falls, WA 98252, 360/691-7791.

7 GOAT FLATS   BEST ◖

in the Boulder River Wilderness of Mount Baker-Snoqualmie
National Forest

🏕 🚶 🏊 🐎 ⛷

Level: Moderate/Strenuous   **Total Distance:** 11.0 miles

Hiking Time: 6 hours   **Elevation Gain:** 2,000 feet

Summary: A rocky and challenging trail climbs past an attractive lake to a mountain meadow paradise and provides access to a lofty fire lookout.

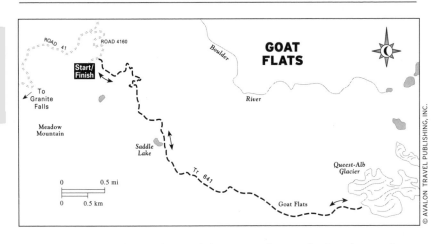

It's hard to believe that such great hiking is so close to the Seattle area. Proximity to the city brings out the crowds, but the high-country beauty of Goat Flats deserves to be experienced by all. Three Fingers Trail travels five miles to the meadowy paradise, where ancient forests surrender to views of old, craggy mountains. This is undoubtedly the best stretch of trail in Boulder River Wilderness.

After miles of clear-cuts along the drive in, Three Fingers Trail wastes no time in entering prime virgin forest. The climb is steady and challenging. Sometimes rocky, sometimes rooty, the trail is in need of repair in several places. Occasionally, you need to grab roots and rocks as handholds. Despite the difficulties, the hike is great. The trail reaches Saddle Lake (2.5 miles), modest in size but inviting nonetheless. This is a refreshing swimming hole, especially on hot days when traveling back down the mountain. There are a few campsites here for those interested.

From Saddle Lake, Three Fingers Trail continues its ascent through the forest before breaking into subalpine meadows. This is the best part of the hike, as the views keep getting better and better. Small streams run from tarn to tarn amongst the meadows of heather and huckleberry. Hikers know they've reached Goat Flats when the trail crests over a particularly wide saddle along the ridge (5.5 miles).

This mountain paradise offers a grand perspective on the Cascades. Three Fingers and Whitehorse frame the end of the Boulder River Valley below. Enjoy the meadows overflowing with flowers in midsummer and the huckleberries in the late summer. Bring your lunch, stick around a while, and you'll be talking about Goat Flats for months.

Options

Three Fingers Trail continues past Goat Flats and climbs to a high fire lookout. This section of trail is challenging, can serve up a good case of vertigo, and is best left for experienced hikers. From Goat Flats, the trail continues climbing and rounds a few minor peaks before reaching Tin Can Gap (6.0 miles). From here, the journey is along a very narrow rock ridge above Queest-Alb Glacier and a set of ladders rising to the lookout. Yes, the views will knock your socks off.

Directions

From Seattle, drive north on I-5 to Everett and turn east on Highway 2. Drive two miles to State Route 204 and head north to Lake Stevens. Drive three

Goat Flats is made up of acres of meadows filled with wildflowers.

miles to State Route 9 and turn left (north). Drive two miles and turn right on State Route 92. Drive eight miles to Granite Falls, where 92 becomes the Mountain Loop Highway. From Granite Falls, drive seven miles east to Tupso Pass Road (Forest Service Road 41). Turn right and drive this long, gravel road to its end, 18 miles later. Watch for road markers, as many small roads branch off the main road, Forest Service Road 41.

Information and Contact

This trail is accessible mid-June–October and is open to hikers and leashed dogs. A federal Northwest Forest Pass is required to park here. For a map of Mount Baker–Snoqualmie National Forest, contact the Outdoor Recreation Information Center at the downtown Seattle REI. For topographic maps, ask Green Trails for No. 109, Granite Falls, and No. 110, Silverton, or ask the USGS for Meadow Mountain and Whitehorse Mountain. For more information, contact Mount Baker–Snoqualmie National Forest, Verlot Public Service Center, 33515 Mountain Loop Highway, Granite Falls, WA 98252, 360/691-7791.

8 HEATHER LAKE

Mount Baker-Snoqualmie National Forest

Level: Easy/Moderate

Hiking Time: 4 hours

Total Distance: 4.7 miles

Elevation Gain: 1,100 feet

Summary: Perfect for all hikers, this easy hike reaches a beautiful lake in a dramatic setting.

Resting at the bottom of Mount Pilchuck's north face, Heather Lake is one of the Mountain Loop Highway's most beautiful day hikes. This route climbs gently and passes through a forest of giant timber before encountering Heather Lake. A well-constructed boardwalk rings the lake, inviting hikers to stick around for a while and enjoy the setting. In the latter part of summer, tasty huckleberries stain your hands while lofty peaks strain your neck. As one of the region's easier trails, Heather Lake is a great hike for hikers of all abilities. For the proximity to the Seattle area and overall grandeur, there are few better destinations.

During the summer, it is immediately apparent at the parking lot that this trail is popular. As one could guess, such an accessible attraction draws the crowds. Hikers visiting Heather Lake in the off-season are more likely to encounter solitude. Although the path is overcome by roots and rocks at times, it is wide enough to easily accommodate the multitudes that hike it.

Heather Lake Trail climbs steadily throughout its length but at an easy grade. From the trailhead, the first mile of trail winds through long-ago-logged land, with enormous cedar stumps testament to the old forests. Notice several 80-foot western hemlocks growing atop cedar stumps, with roots snaking to the ground. Soon, the trail enters virgin forest (0.9 mile) set upon steep slopes, and one can understand why this forest was saved. The steep cliffs formed a difficult challenge to the lumberjacks working this valley. Large western hemlock and western red cedar fill the old forest. In the spring, the forest is filled with the sounds of songbirds.

Heather Lake Trail continues climbing through this great stretch of trail as the loud rush of Heather Creek filters up from the valley to the right. The trail reaches the crest of the hike (1.6 miles) and drops into Heather Lake Basin. Here, Mount Pilchuck's tall, steep walls form much of the horizon and create a protected sanctuary. The trail makes a loop around the lake with the help of numerous wooden structures to keep your feet dry. Time your hike right (in August), and you can enjoy a rich feast of berries. Although it's not much of a swimming hole, Heather Lake is a fine place for fishing.

Directions

From Seattle, drive north on I-5 to Everett and turn east on Highway 2. Drive two miles to State Route 204 and head north to Lake Stevens. Drive three miles to State Route 9 and turn left (north). Drive two miles and turn right on State Route 92. Drive eight miles to Granite Falls, where 92 becomes the Mountain Loop Highway. From Granite Falls, drive east 12 miles on the Mountain Loop Highway to Pilchuck Road (Forest Service Road 42). Turn right and drive 1.5 miles to the signed trailhead.

Information and Contact

This trail is accessible mid-May–November and is open to hikers and leashed dogs. A federal Northwest Forest Pass is required to park here. For a map of Mount Baker–Snoqualmie National Forest, contact the Outdoor Recreation Information Center at the downtown Seattle REI. For topographic maps, ask Green Trails for No. 109, Granite Falls, or ask the USGS for Verlot. For more information, contact Mount Baker–Snoqualmie National Forest, Verlot Public Service Center, 33515 Mountain Loop Highway, Granite Falls, WA 98252, 360/691-7791.

9 MOUNT PILCHUCK

Mount Baker-Snoqualmie National Forest and
Mount Pilchuck State Park

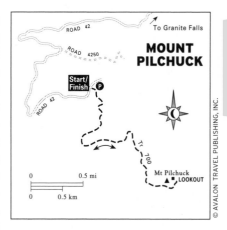

Level: Moderate   **Total Distance:** 5.8 miles

Hiking Time: 3 hours   **Elevation Gain:** 2,200 feet

Summary: A scenic and popular hike to a fire lookout with knock-out views of Puget Sound.

From start to finish, Mount Pilchuck Trail is a great hike. But the grandest attraction is undoubtedly the restored fire lookout at the summit. Built in 1920, the lookout was restored by the Everett Chapter of the Mountaineers to a condition equaling the outstanding views from within. The lookout peers out over the Puget Sound Basin to the west and over countless North Cascade peaks to the east. The lookout contains a full history of the site, old photographs of the region, as well as a great map of visible peaks. This is on top of a hike through a beautiful old-growth forest and parkland meadows among the granite slabs of the mountain. Getting to Mount Pilchuck is a breeze. It's the Mountain Loop Highway's closest, easiest-to-access trail from Seattle. Perfect for hikers of all abilities, Mount Pilchuck is a grand excursion for a day hike.

Mount Pilchuck Trail begins within a forest teeming with giant western hemlocks. After crossing several streams, the trail gets down to business and begins climbing steadily. The trail is sometimes rocky, so a pair of tennis shoes won't cut it—hikers wearing boots that cover the ankles will fare better. Making a turn to the east in a field of talus (1.1 miles), the trail enters open meadows, awash in wildflowers in June and views of the Stillaguamish Valley year-round, weather permitting.

The trail gradually turns to the right and works its way around Little Pilchuck to enter the north basin (1.7 miles). Hemlocks and Alaskan yellow cedar find ground amid enormous slabs of granite. Snow lingers well into summer along this north-facing basin, although it rarely poses a problem for hikers.

The ascent to the summit is the steepest part of the route, as the trail follows the ridgeline up to the lookout shelter (2.8 miles). Kick back, relax, and enjoy a snack atop the summit. On a sunny day, there is no grander view of the Puget Sound Basin. The view includes glittering Puget Sound and the San Juan Islands; to the north and east are countless Cascade peaks. Check the weather before heading out, as Pilchuck has a nasty reputation for fast-arriving fog, which can quickly turn a beautiful view into a slow hike back to the car. Mount Pilchuck sees its fair share of hikers during the off-season and on weekdays, not to mention summer weekends, which can be downright packed.

Directions
From Seattle, drive north on I-5 to Everett and turn east on Highway 2. Drive two miles to State Route 204 and head north to Lake Stevens. Drive three miles to State Route 9 and turn left (north). Drive two miles and turn right on State Route 92. Drive eight miles to Granite Falls, where 92 becomes the Mountain Loop Highway. From Granite Falls, drive east 12 miles on the Mountain Loop Highway to Pilchuck Road (Forest Service Road 42). Turn right and drive seven miles to the signed trailhead at road's end.

Information and Contact
This trail is accessible April–November and is open to hikers and leashed dogs. A federal Northwest Forest Pass is required to park here. Leashed dogs are allowed, but horses and mountain bikes are not. There is no wheelchair access. For a map of Mount Baker–Snoqualmie National Forest, contact the Outdoor Recreation Information Center at the downtown Seattle REI. For topographic maps, ask Green Trails for No. 109, Granite Falls, or ask the USGS for Verlot. For more information, contact Mount Baker–Snoqualmie National Forest, Verlot Public Service Center, 33515 Mountain Loop Highway, Granite Falls, WA 98252, 360/691-7791.

10 LAKE 22   BEST [

Mount Baker-Snoqualmie National Forest

Level: Moderate

Total Distance: 6.4 miles

Hiking Time: 4 hours

Elevation Gain: 1,400 feet

Summary: Scenic waterfalls and virgin old-growth forest make this a Mountain Loop Highway favorite.

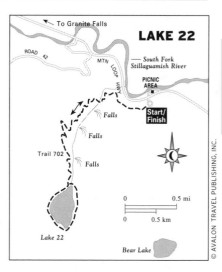

The designation of Lake 22 Research Natural Area preserved the landscape around this trail, making it a jewel of the southern Mountain Loop Highway. Climbing entirely through old-growth forest, the journey is as beautiful as the destination, which is a tall order in Lake 22's case. Along the trail, cascading waterfalls work to draw your attention from enormous Douglas firs and western red cedars. At the lake, steep walls leading to a rugged ridge of granite vie for your attention with fields of huckleberry bushes.

Although challenging, Lake 22 is an accessible hike for many people. The route gains just 1,400 feet on a steady but not difficult grade. Switchbacks help to minimize the incline, but many folks still find the trail to be a workout. This trail has seen much recent trail work, including the construction of a one-mile loop around the lake. Work centered on compacting the trail tread to limit erosion and protect many rare plant species found in the Research Natural Area (RNA). This work has also helped to ease the impact of the above-average use that the trail sees.

Lake 22 Trail leaves the parking lot and rambles briefly along the bottom of the Stillaguamish Valley. Before long, it begins heading up the slopes of Mount Pilchuck (0.6 mile) with 22 Creek a regular companion, rumbling beside the trail with several large cascades. The tread is well-maintained, and the number of log structures is impressive.

After crossing 22 Creek (0.8 mile), switchbacks become the major theme. As they zigzag up the hillside, they pass beneath enormous old-growth

old-growth trees in the protected Lake 22 Research Natural Area

hemlocks and cedars. The cool shade breaks as the trail passes through several open talus fields overgrown with vine maple and corn lily. Lake 22 receives as much as 15 feet of snow during the winter, meaning that winter trips to the lake require snowshoes.

Just when you've lost count of the number of switchbacks, the grade crosses a small hump and Lake 22 stands before you (2.7 miles), guarded by the towering north face of Mount Pilchuck. The lake is stocked, so a fishing pole can be put to good use here. The new loop circles the lake and offers several nice swimming holes. This is a great day hike from Seattle and is very popular, but no size of crowd should keep hikers from experiencing Lake 22.

Please take note that dogs are not allowed on the trail and camping is not permitted at the lake. Because this hike lies within a Research Natural Area, priority is given to preservation rather than recreational use.

Directions

From Seattle, drive north on I-5 to Everett and turn east on Highway 2. Drive two miles to State Route 204 and head north to Lake Stevens. Drive three miles to State Route 9 and turn left (north). Drive two miles and turn right on State Route 92. Drive eight miles to Granite Falls, where 92 becomes the Mountain Loop Highway. From Granite Falls, drive east 13 miles on the Mountain Loop Highway (Highway 530) to the signed trailhead on the right.

Information and Contact
This trail is accessible May–November. Dogs are not allowed on the trail. A federal Northwest Forest Pass is required to park here. For a map of Mount Baker–Snoqualmie National Forest, contact the Outdoor Recreation Information Center at the downtown Seattle REI. For topographic maps, ask Green Trails for No. 109, Granite Falls, or ask the USGS for Verlot and Mallardy Ridge. For more information, contact Mount Baker–Snoqualmie National Forest, Verlot Public Service Center, 33515 Mountain Loop Highway, Granite Falls, WA 98252, 360/691-7791.

11 ASHLAND LAKES

south of Verlot on Washington Department of Natural Resources land

Level: Easy/Moderate

Hiking Time: 4 hours

Total Distance: 9.2 miles

Elevation Gain: 1,200 feet

Summary: An easy hike through old forest to four lakes and a dramatic waterfall.

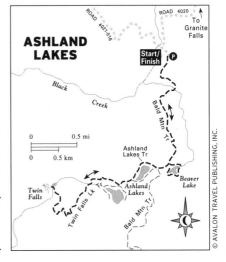

The trail to Ashland Lakes and Twin Falls is one of the Seattle area's lesser-known hikes. Consequently, there are rarely many other hikers on the trail. That's a shame, since this is a great family hike to four lakes and several waterfalls. Located on Washington Department of Natural Resources land, which is usually not very scenic, the Ashland Lakes area actually retains its old-growth forests and meadows. Perhaps the nickname Department of Nothing Left is not entirely appropriate after all.

The hike to Ashland Lakes gets off to a less-than-spectacular start—from the parking area at the end of the road you have to walk one mile to the signed beginning of Bald Mountain Trail. From here the hiking is much better. The trail encounters a turnoff for Beaver Lake (2.0 miles). The short loop trail makes its way around the small, forested lake—it's worth checking out on a leisurely day. By now you've noticed that much of the trail is wooden boardwalks or planks. Take care when walking on these structures, as they are extremely slippery when wet.

Just after Beaver Lake is another junction (2.2 miles) where Bald Mountain Trail begins to climb its namesake. Stay to the left on Ashland Lakes Trail and soon encounter Upper Ashland Lake (2.3 miles). The trail diverges around the lake and meets up on the other side. Lower Ashland Lake is just beyond (2.9 miles). Both Ashland Lakes are okay swimming holes and have picnic sites. Keep in mind that the trail from Lower Ashland Lake to Twin Falls drops 700 feet, so Lower Ashland Lake may be an ideal turnaround point for some families.

Beyond Lower Ashland Lake, the trail becomes Twin Falls Lake Trail and

© CHRIS DUVAL

Twin Falls cascades into the fourth and final lake on Ashland Lakes Trail.

drops quickly to the fourth and final lake of the hike (4.6 miles). Here several waterfalls on Wilson Creek make large drops, including a dramatic cascade into Twin Falls Lake. Again, there are camp and picnic sites around the lake, the best swimming hole of the hike.

Directions
From Seattle, drive north on I-5 to Everett and head east on Highway 2. In just a few miles, turn east on Highway 204. Drive east to Lake Stevens and turn north on State Route 9. Turn right on State Route 92 and drive to Granite Falls. Drive straight through downtown and turn left on Mountain Loop Highway. Drive 4.5 miles east of Verlot to Forest Service Road 4020. Turn right (south) and drive 2.3 miles to Forest Service Road 4021. Turn right and drive 1.5 miles to Forest Service Road 4021-016. Turn left onto Forest Service Road 4021-016 and drive to the Ashland trailhead at road's end.

Information and Contact
This trail is accessible May–November and is open to hikers and leashed dogs—no horses or mountain bikes are allowed. A federal Northwest Forest Pass is required to park here. For a map of this area, contact the Outdoor Recreation Information Center at the downtown Seattle REI. For topographic maps, ask Green Trails for No. 110, Silverton, and No. 142, Index, or ask the USGS for Mallardy Ridge. For more information, contact Mount Baker–Snoqualmie National Forest, Verlot Public Service Center, 33515 Mountain Loop Highway, Granite Falls, WA 98252, 360/691-7791.

12 CUTTHROAT LAKES

Mount Pilchuck Natural Resources Conservation Area

🏕 🌸 🔦 🐕 🎿

Level: Moderate   **Total Distance:** 8.4 miles

Hiking Time: 5 hours   **Elevation Gain:** 1,300 feet

Summary: An incredible hike through old-growth forest and meadows to a collection of beautiful lakes.

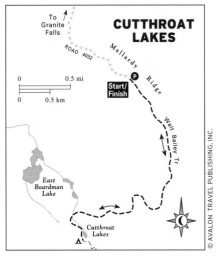

Walt Bailey Trail to Cutthroat Lakes is a gem of the Mountain Loop Highway. The scenery is outstanding, considering the trail barely rises above 4,000 feet elevation. Cutting through several meadows, the trail ends up at one of the prettiest subalpine lake basins around. Such a great trip is not without its difficulties, however. The trail is more challenging than the elevation gain would imply; several elevation losses create extra climbing. At times the trail is rocky, ripped up by roots, steep, or all three. Good boots are a must. Regardless, the hike is a dandy. Few trails match the diversity of scenery on the hike to Cutthroat Lakes.

Walt Bailey Trail begins by gently climbing along the side of Mallardy Ridge. After a short ascent, the trail crosses several small streams (1.0 mile). This is the start of regularly appearing meadows, full of blooming marsh marigolds and shooting stars in June and juicy huckleberries in August. The trail drops and enters another meadow before rounding an open avalanche chute (2.0 miles).

The most challenging segment of the trail lies just ahead (at 2.5 miles), where the trail begins a steep climb into the Cutthroat Lakes Basin. This section of trail is one of the rockiest. With high levels of traffic, the tread has been beaten into muddy steps at places. The hard work is over when the trail crests into open meadows (3.9 miles).

The trail wanders through a rocky landscape where Cutthroat Lakes lie scattered about. Some are more tarns than lakes, while others are quite large.

The trail drops to several established campsites beside one of the larger lakes (4.2 miles). Open meadows and solitary mountain hemlocks blanket the large basin. Above, the rocky peak of Bald Mountain watches over the basin. This area has seen lots of use and even a little abuse. It's important to walk only on established trails in the basin. The subalpine setting is testament to the harsh conditions, even at 3,800 feet.

approaching Cutthroat Lakes and the main campsites

Options

For hikers with extra ambition, a trip to the saddle below Bald Mountain is a worthwhile extension. The saddle reveals new views of peaks within the Skykomish Valley. Even the skyline of Seattle appears on the distant horizon. From the camp at Cutthroat Lakes, follow a well-worn trail as it rises to the high saddle above the lake basin, 1.2 miles from the lake. The trail becomes brushy and is very lightly used as it continues along the south side of Bald Mountain.

Directions

From Seattle, drive north on I-5 to Everett and head east on Highway 2. In just a few miles, turn east on Highway 204. Drive east to Lake Stevens and turn north on State Route 9. Turn right on State Route 92 and drive to Granite Falls. Drive straight through downtown and turn left on Mountain Loop Highway. Drive 18 miles, past Verlot, to Mallardy Road, Forest Service Road 4030. This is just before passing Red Bridge and its campground. Turn right and drive 1.3 miles to Forest Service Road 4032. Veer right and drive 5.7 miles to the signed trailhead. Parking space is limited. On busy days, expect to park away from the trailhead, on the roadside.

Information and Contact

This trail is accessible May–October and is open to hikers and leashed dogs. A federal Northwest Forest Pass is required to park here. For a map of Mount

Baker–Snoqualmie National Forest, contact the Outdoor Recreation Information Center at the downtown Seattle REI. For topographic maps, ask Green Trails for No. 110, Silverton, or ask the USGS for Mallardy Ridge. For more information, contact Mount Baker–Snoqualmie National Forest, Verlot Public Service Center, 33515 Mountain Loop Highway, Granite Falls, WA 98252, 360/691-7791.

1 3 BIG FOUR ICE CAVES

Mount Baker-Snoqualmie National Forest

Level: Easy

Hiking Time: 1 hour

Total Distance: 2.0 miles

Elevation Gain: 200 feet

Summary: An easy walk to the base of towering Big Four Mountain where avalanches annually build up large ice caves.

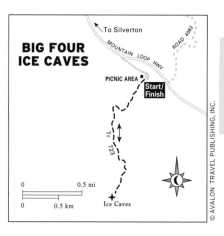

Big Four Ice Caves is an ideal hike for families. Even for the serious hiker, this is a cool side trip. An easy trail leads to a set of ice caves at the base of the towering cliffs of Big Four Mountain. To catch the ice caves, you have to hit the trail at the right time of year, since this natural phenomenon only lasts a few months. The caves usually form by June and last well into August, sometimes all the way to October. The health of the previous snow year is the biggest factor in determining their staying power. When the caves are present, late afternoons are filled with the rumble of the ice breaking apart.

The caves are created when snow slides off Big Four Mountain and piles up at the base. Spring runoff creates small caves inside the ice which are eventually enlarged by warm air flowing through the cavities. As scenic as the ice caves may be, this can be a dangerous place. The winter season is best left alone—avalanches are a regular occurrence well into March. During the summer, the caves are continually melting and eventually collapse. Climbing on or hiking into the ice caves is not recommended. From a distance (the trail), a visit to the ice caves is very safe.

The trail is accessed by either Big Four trailhead or Big Four Ice Caves Picnic Area. The two trails meet up within a few hundred yards of each other, so either trailhead is fine. From where the trails meet up (0.1 mile), Big Four Ice Caves Trail crosses the Stillaguamish River on a large bridge and quickly crosses Ice Creek on another wooden span (0.3 mile). The trail gently meanders up a small incline and crosses Ice Creek on the hike's third great bridge (0.8 mile).

Suddenly, the forest turns into a large blowdown of timber (0.9 mile). The trees all point away from the mountain—enormous avalanches each winter scour and ravage the trees. Immediately beyond is the trail's terminus at the ice caves (1.0 mile). Waterfalls tumble down the sheer cliffs of Big Four Mountain, rising more than 4,000 feet straight up. To the north, Stillaguamish Peak and Mount Forgotten are visible. Even if the ice caves have melted, this is an impressive vantage.

Directions

From Seattle, drive north on I-90 to Everett and turn east on Highway 2. Drive two miles and turn east on Highway 204 to Lake Stevens. Drive three miles and turn north on Highway 9 to Lake Stevens. Drive two miles and turn east on Highway

The ice caves vary in size – in the summer many are melted out.

92. Drive nine miles straight through the town of Granite Falls. At the end of town, turn left on the Mountain Loop Highway (signed to Verlot and Darrington). Drive 26 miles east on the Mountain Loop Highway, through the towns of Verlot and Silverton, to the signed Big Four Ice Caves trailhead. The Big Four Ice Caves Picnic Area, a half mile before the trailhead, also accesses the Ice Caves and is an okay place to park.

Information and Contact

This trail is accessible May–October and is open to hikers and leashed dogs. A federal Northwest Forest Pass is required to park here. For a map of Mount Baker–Snoqualmie National Forest, contact the Outdoor Recreation Information Center at the downtown Seattle REI. For topographic maps, ask Green Trails for No. 111, Sloan Peak, and No. 143, Monte Cristo, or ask the USGS for Silverton. For more information, contact Mount Baker–Snoqualmie National Forest, Verlot Public Service Center, 33515 Mountain Loop Highway, Granite Falls, WA 98252, 360/691-7791.

14 MOUNT FORGOTTEN MEADOWS   BEST 【

Mount Baker-Snoqualmie National Forest

🏕 🌲 🐾 🎿

Level: Moderate/Strenuous

Total Distance: 8.0 miles

Hiking Time: 5 hours

Elevation Gain: 3,000 feet

Summary: A demanding hike through old-growth forest to a spectacular meadow with panoramic views of the Cascades.

The trails seem to get better and better as one drives farther back into the Stillaguamish Valley. Miles from civilization, the lush green forest gives way to steep slopes rising to glacier-capped peaks. It's back here, tucked away in the mass of mountains ringed by the Mountain Loop Highway, where hikers can find the excellent hike to Mount Forgotten Meadows. Although Perry Creek Trail is challenging, it delivers one of the best views within the Mountain Loop Highway Corridor.

Perry Creek Trail climbs to Mount Forgotten Meadows and has two distinct segments. From the trailhead, the trail climbs steadily at a gentle grade through leafy forests and exposed talus fields. Perry Creek rumbles below the trail, sometimes within view and always within earshot. The trail can be fairly rocky at times, particularly around the talus fields. Hiking boots with good support will save many a sore ankle on this trail.

Perry Creek soon approaches an old forest of tall fir trees where it cascades over a large waterfall. Unfortunately, a good view of the fall is obscured by the forest and surrounding rock. The trail crosses the creek (1.9 miles) and quickly becomes mean. Switchbacks ruthlessly ascend the steep slope beneath old-growth Alaskan yellow cedars and Pacific silver firs. In August, huckleberry bushes encourage regular rest breaks. The trail climbs a total of 3,000 feet, a considerable elevation change. Extra water is an important provision on hot summer days, which quickly take their toll despite the forest shade.

The miles of climbing are worth every step when the trail breaks out of the forest onto the open ridge between Stillaguamish Peak and Mount Forgotten

(3.9 miles). From here, Mount Forgotten stares down on you, and great mountain views are finally at hand. But the best is yet to come. Just before the pass, which is accessed on an unofficial but obvious trail, Perry Creek Trail cuts to the right and comes to an end in the expansive meadows beneath Mount Forgotten (4.0 miles). July is a great time to catch the acres of wildflowers in full bloom.

Panoramic views offer up countless North Cascades peaks. The rocky crag of Mount Forgotten Peak lies directly to the north, a popular peak with rock climbers. On a clear day, it seems as though one can reach out and touch Glacier Peak. With numerous outcroppings of granite making for great picnic benches, long lunches are highly encouraged.

Directions

From Seattle, drive north on I-5 to Everett and turn east on Highway 2. Drive two miles to State Route 204 and head north to Lake Stevens. Drive three miles to State Route 9 and turn left (north). Drive two miles and turn right on State Route 92. Drive eight miles to Granite Falls, where 92 becomes the Mountain Loop Highway. From Granite Falls, drive east 26 miles on Mountain Loop Highway (Highway 530) to Perry Creek Road (Forest Service Road 4063). Turn left and drive 1.5 miles (stay left at the fork) to the trailhead at road's end.

© PATTI BLEIFUSS

On a clear day, Glacier Peak is visible from Mount Forgotten Meadows.

Information and Contact

This trail is accessible June–October and is open to hikers and leashed dogs. A federal Northwest Forest Pass is required to park here. For a map of Mount Baker–Snoqualmie National Forest, contact the Outdoor Recreation Information Center at the downtown Seattle REI. For topographic maps, ask Green Trails for No. 111, Sloan Peak, or ask the USGS for Bedal. For more information, contact Mount Baker–Snoqualmie National Forest, Verlot Public Service Center, 33515 Mountain Loop Highway, Granite Falls, WA 98252, 360/691-7791.

15 MOUNT DICKERMAN   BEST **C**

Mount Baker-Snoqualmie National Forest

Level: Strenuous   **Total Distance:** 9.2 miles

Hiking Time: 8 hours   **Elevation Gain:** 4,000 feet

Summary: A grinder of a climb through forest and blueberry patches to an outstanding summit.

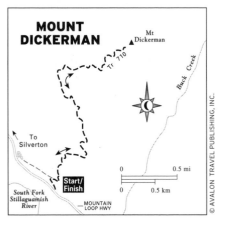

Mount Dickerman persists as a Mountain Loop Highway favorite in spite of its punishing nature. After all, prolific berry bushes and expansive mountain views have the tendency to cancel out killer ascents. During the burly hike up countless switchbacks, keep your mind focused on the August berries that will surely revive your step. And during the final rise, keep your attention on the opening and expanding scenes, culminated by a near orgy of views at the summit. Mount Dickerman can be a busy trail in the summer, but as always with North Cascade summits, it's well worth it.

Mount Dickerman Trail starts off mean and only gets meaner. After a quick traverse of the hillside, the trail begins a relentless series of switchbacks. The grade may not be difficult, but it never ceases climbing. Back and forth the trail zigzags up the mountain, quickly putting elevation beneath your feet. Fortunately, the trail stays beneath the cool shade of the forest canopy and a few seasonal streams are refreshing breaks. Nonetheless, packing extra water and snacks is a wise foresight. The trail momentarily eases up as the grade levels out in the thinning forest (2.8 miles).

From here, Mount Dickerman Trail is absolutely spectacular. The hike enters open meadows chock-full of blueberry bushes, ripe for the picking in August. In the fall, the blazing colors of the bushes contrast beautifully against a light snowfall. Slow travel along this stretch of trail is common as the views get better with every step. The final ascent is another series of taxing switchbacks. For your effort, Mount Dickerman rewards quite well. The panoramic views from the summit (4.6 miles) are as good as they get in the area. Glacier

© PATTI BLEIFUSS

The views from atop Mount Dickerman are some of the best in the Cascades.

Peak, Monte Cristo, Sloan Peak, and countless other lofty mountains quickly fill the camera with snapshots.

Directions

From Seattle, drive north on I-90 to Everett and turn east on Highway 2. Drive two miles and turn east on Highway 204 to Lake Stevens. Drive three miles and turn north on Highway 9 to Lake Stevens. Drive two miles and turn east on Highway 92. Drive nine miles straight through the town of Granite Falls. At the end of town, turn left on the Mountain Loop Highway (signed to Verlot and Darrington). Drive 28 miles east on the Mountain Loop Highway, through the towns of Verlot and Silverton to the signed parking lot and trailhead on the left (north) side of the road.

Information and Contact

This trail is accessible July–October and is open to hikers and leashed dogs. A federal Northwest Forest Pass is required to park here. For a map of Mount Baker–Snoqualmie National Forest, contact the Outdoor Recreation Information Center at the downtown Seattle REI. For topographic maps, ask Green Trails for No. 111, Sloan Peak, or ask the USGS for Bedal. For more information, contact Mount Baker–Snoqualmie National Forest, Verlot Public Service Center, 33515 Mountain Loop Highway, Granite Falls, WA 98252, 360/691-7791.

16 GOTHIC BASIN   BEST ◖

in the Henry M. Jackson Wilderness of Mount Baker-Snoqualmie
National Forest

Level: Strenuous   **Total Distance:** 9.0 miles

Hiking Time: 8 hours   **Elevation Gain:** 2,600 feet

Summary: A strenuous, knee-busting hike to large Gothic Basin and several lakes, the best of the Henry M. Jackson Wilderness.

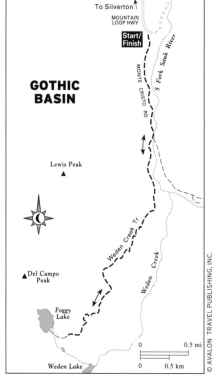

While little remains of the once-bustling mining town of Monte Cristo, the miners' trails live on. The trail up to Gothic Basin, one of many mines in the area, reveals the job's greatest perk: unbelievable views of mountains and valleys. Indeed, Gothic Basin Trail is a testament to the hardiness of the old miners. In a successful effort to get to the work site quickly, it makes a very steep ascent to the basin, a barren moonscape save for large Foggy Lake and other tarns. The overall length and elevation gain don't do justice to the real difficulty of this hike. The first mile is on Monte Cristo Road, which is open to bicycles—this is a potential bike-and-hike combo.

Monte Cristo Road follows the South Fork Sauk River to Weden Creek Trail, which is signed and located on the right immediately before the road crosses the river (1.1 miles). Turn right on Weden Creek Trail, the main route, as it gently traverses the hillside to a trouble-free creek crossing (1.6 miles). This is the last of the easy stuff—everything beyond is strenuous. The trail brutally switchbacks up the mountainside and very quickly gains elevation. This section is forested by big trees—the shade is especially welcome on sunny summer days.

The trail breaks out of the forest and reaches a large creek as it cascades from Del Campo Peak (3.0 miles). This is the first of many great views. The trail becomes very rocky and makes for slow going, especially on the way down. There are several more creek crossings, and each can harbor snow well into August. When they do, take exceptional care in crossing them. An ice ax is recommended in early summer—by mid-summer it isn't necessary.

After the last of the sketchy creek crossings (3.5 miles), the trail gets meaner and shoots quickly up to a pass and Gothic Basin (4.5 miles) in an expansive bowl of heather meadows. The trail ends at a small lake—side trails explore the basin. A popular short trip is straight up the back of the basin to Foggy Lake where Del Campo and Gothic Peaks tower above on either side. For the rock hounds out there, this is a great place to explore. Numerous types of rocks are found up here, including conglomerates, granite, limestone, and sandstone. It's amazing to think that this place used to be, for miners, just another day at the office.

Directions

From Seattle, drive north on I-90 to Everett and turn east on Highway 2. Drive two miles and turn east on Highway 204 to Lake Stevens. Drive three miles and turn north on Highway 9 to Lake Stevens. Drive two miles and turn east on Highway 92. Drive nine miles straight through the town of Granite Falls.

Del Campo Peak towers over Gothic Basin.

At the end of town, turn left on the Mountain Loop Highway (signed to Verlot and Darrington). Drive 30 miles east on the Mountain Loop Highway, through the towns of Verlot and Silverton, to the signed trailhead at Barlow Pass, where the pavement ends and the gravel begins.

Information and Contact

This trail is accessible mid-July–October and is open to hikers, leashed dogs, and mountain bikes (on Monte Cristo Road only). A federal Northwest Forest Pass is required to park here. For a map of Mount Baker–Snoqualmie National Forest, contact the Outdoor Recreation Information Center at the downtown Seattle REI. For topographic maps, ask Green Trails for No. 111, Sloan Peak, and No. 143, Monte Cristo, or ask the USGS for Bedal and Monte Cristo. For more information, contact Mount Baker–Snoqualmie National Forest, Verlot Public Service Center, 33515 Mountain Loop Highway, Granite Falls, WA 98252, 360/691-7791.

17 GLACIER BASIN

in the Henry M. Jackson Wilderness of Mount Baker-Snoqualmie National Forest

Level: Moderate/Strenuous

Total Distance: 12.4 miles

Hiking Time: 8 hours

Elevation Gain: 2,100 feet

Summary: After an easy road hike to the old Monte Cristo town site, this trail climbs steeply to enormous Glacier Basin beneath giant mountains.

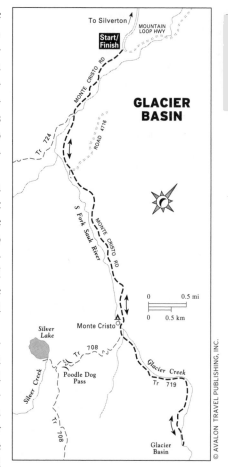

Glacier Basin has the ability to make a person feel about as big as an ant. With massive mountains towering several thousand feet above the basin on every side, any understanding of perspective slips off into the thin mountain air. The imposing cliffs and peaks of Cadet and Monte Cristo seem to redefine scale. Glacier Basin is the perfect locale to reset the human ego.

The hike to Glacier Basin is an ideal bike-and-hike combo. The first 4.1 miles travel along the old Monte Cristo Road, which is now closed to motor vehicle traffic. Instead of walking this distance (and back again), I recommend taking a mountain bike and biking to the trailhead at the old Monte Cristo town site.

Monte Cristo was a thriving mining town around the turn of the 20th century. Hundreds of workers mined the towering mountains for gold during the day and raised hell at night in this rugged frontier town. Today, only remnants of the town remain, but there are still many relics, including some old buildings and a locomotive turntable. A trip to only the town site is recommended for people seeking an easy day hike (400 feet elevation gain in 4.1 miles).

From the parking lot at Barlow Pass, head south on the gated and signed Monte Cristo Road. At 1.1 miles, the road crosses the South Fork of the Sauk River at Twin Bridges. The road ends at Monte Cristo town site—walk through the town to the signed Glacier Basin Trail on the left. This is the beginning of trail proper and the workout. The trail starts off at a decent pace before sharply quickening in its ascent. Many sections of the trail are rocky and rugged—good hiking boots are a must. Rising up the valley, the trail passes a dramatic waterfall on Glacier Creek before taking a turn up over Mystery Hill (6.0 miles), the place for overnight camps.

By now the forest has faded away and meadows fill in between talus slopes. Picas and marmots are heard frequently, just before they scuttle off beneath the rocks. The trail gradually levels out and enters the basin (6.2 miles), which is filled with meadows and interlocked braids of creeks. This is beautiful alpine territory, not so long ago buried beneath massive glaciers. Cadet, Monte Cristo, and Wilmon Peaks surround the large basin.

Directions

From Seattle, drive north on I-90 to Everett and turn east on Highway 2. Drive two miles and turn east on Highway 204 to Lake Stevens. Drive three miles and turn north on Highway 9 to Lake Stevens. Drive two miles and turn east on Highway 92. Drive nine miles straight through the town of Granite Falls. At the end of town, turn left on the Mountain Loop Highway (signed to Verlot and Darrington). Drive 30 miles east on the Mountain Loop Highway, through the towns of Verlot and Silverton, to the signed trailhead at Barlow Pass, where the pavement ends and the gravel begins.

Information and Contact

This trail is accessible July–October and is open to hikers, leashed dogs, and mountain bikes (on Monte Cristo Road only). A federal Northwest Forest Pass is required to park here. For a map of Mount Baker–Snoqualmie National Forest, contact the Outdoor Recreation Information Center at the downtown Seattle REI. For topographic maps, ask Green Trails for No. 111, Sloan Peak, and No. 143, Monte Cristo, or ask the USGS for Bedal, Monte Cristo, and Blanca Lake. For more information, contact Mount Baker–Snoqualmie National Forest, Verlot Public Service Center, 33515 Mountain Loop Highway, Granite Falls, WA 98252, 360/691-7791.

18 POODLE DOG PASS AND SILVER LAKE

in the Henry M. Jackson Wilderness of Mount Baker-Snoqualmie National Forest

Level: Moderate

Hiking Time: 8 hours

Total Distance: 12.2 miles

Elevation Gain: 2,200 feet

Summary: An easy walk to the old mining town of Monte Cristo before a sharp climb up rugged peaks and mountains to meadows and a lake with beautiful views.

Silver Lake at Poodle Dog Pass is a typically beautiful but challenging Mountain Loop Highway hike and is set deep within the Cascades. After a four-mile trek on gravel road, Silver Lake Trail climbs to Silver Lake at Poodle Dog Pass. This is high country, where meadows of heather cover the hillsides and mountain peaks dominate the skyline. The closure of Monte Cristo Road makes this a long trek, but it offers a good bike-and-hike combo and also helps shoo away crowds. Rugged peaks and mountains are the theme to this hike, one of the best of the Monte Cristo region. The hike also offers a longer option to little-visited Twin Lakes.

Accessing Poodle Dog Pass requires an easy four-mile hike or bike down Monte Cristo Road. Although the road is closed to vehicles, it's not closed to mountain bikes, an easy way to turn eight miles of less-than-thrilling road hiking into a fun bike ride. The hike to Monte Cristo is a fun and much easier alternative to trudging up to Silver Lake (400 feet elevation gain

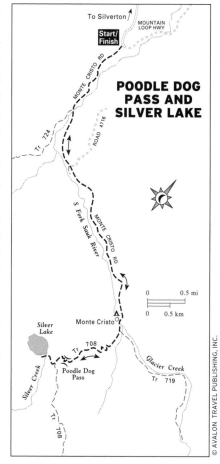

POODLE DOG PASS AND SILVER LAKE

© AVALON TRAVEL PUBLISHING, INC.

in 4.1 miles). Monte Cristo was a thriving mining town around the turn of the 20th century. Today, only remnants of the town remain but there are still many relics, including old wooden buildings and a locomotive turntable.

From the parking lot at Barlow Pass, begin on the gated and signed Monte Cristo Road, crossing the South Fork Sauk River at Twin Bridges (1.1 miles). The road reaches a junction at Monte Cristo Campground (4.0 miles). Take a right at this junction and walk through town. After crossing a small bridge, take a right on signed Silver Lake Trail (4.1 miles). This is the start of real hiking trail and also where the trail finally becomes difficult.

From Monte Cristo, Poodle Dog Pass Trail steadily climbs out of the forest and into meadows, climbing over 1,600 feet in just 1.7 miles. Although the trail has been rebuilt relatively recently, it is rugged and rocky in some places—good hiking boots are a plus. The grade finally flattens upon arrival at Poodle Dog Pass and a junction (5.8 miles). Take a right and drop slightly to Silver Lake (6.1 miles). Meadows and picnic spots surround the lake, while Silvertip Peak towers above the blue waters.

Options
Twin Lakes is an added 2.7 miles one-way from Poodle Dog Pass. It's not difficult if you bike along Monte Cristo Road but can be a very long day if hiking the whole way. From Poodle Dog Pass (5.8 miles), take a left on Twin Lakes Trail as it continues through superb terrain of meadows and rock fields. The trail shoots right between Twin Peaks (7.8 miles) before dropping to Twin Lakes (8.5 miles). The long ridge of Columbia Peak stands more than 2,400 feet above the lakes, creating a large, ringed basin.

Directions
From Seattle, drive north on I-90 to Everett and turn east on Highway 2. Drive two miles and turn east on Highway 204 to Lake Stevens. Drive three miles and turn north on Highway 9 to Lake Stevens. Drive two miles and turn east on Highway 92. Drive nine miles straight through the town of Granite Falls. At the end of town, turn left on the Mountain Loop Highway (signed to Verlot and Darrington). Drive 30 miles east on the Mountain Loop Highway, through the towns of Verlot and Silverton, to the signed trailhead at Barlow Pass, where the pavement ends and the gravel begins.

Information and Contact
This trail is accessible July–October and is open to hikers, leashed dogs, and mountain bikes (on Monte Cristo Road only). A federal Northwest Forest Pass

is required to park here. For a map of Mount Baker–Snoqualmie National Forest, contact the Outdoor Recreation Information Center at the downtown Seattle REI. For topographic maps, ask Green Trails for No. 111, Sloan Peak, and No. 143, Monte Cristo, or ask the USGS for Bedal and Monte Cristo. For more information, contact Mount Baker–Snoqualmie National Forest, Verlot Public Service Center, 33515 Mountain Loop Highway, Granite Falls, WA 98252, 360/691-7791.

HIGHWAY 2

© SCOTT LEONARD

BEST HIKES

Highway 2, which travels up to the beautiful
Skykomish River Valley, Stevens Pass, and onward to Leavenworth and Wenatchee, is very close to Seattle and a popular destination for day hikers, yet it does not see the crowds of the hikes near I-90. Framed by steep valley walls and rugged snowcapped peaks shaped by intense glacial carving, the Skykomish River Valley is chock-full of high mountain lakes. The trails to these lakes dominate this chapter and many of them require moderate or strenuous efforts, though a few trails make great family outings.

Ten of the thirteen hikes listed in this chapter visit one or more lakes on the trail. Two nice lake hikes are located in the Sultan River Basin, a tributary to the Skykomish. Boulder Lake is a scenic, wild, and rarely visited lake beneath big cliffs. Greider Lakes are a pair of low-elevation lakes that are accessed by a short but very steep trail.

Back out on the Skykomish River, the lakes continue to abound. The hike to Lake Serene passes Bridal Veil Falls on the way to the scenic lake beneath towering Mount Index. Surprise Lake Trail is a decent climb to its namesake and is a popular hike in the valley. Foss Lakes and Necklace Valley are Skykomish classics, climbing up to big basins filled with numerous mountain lakes. The trip to Snoqualmie Lake is less difficult but no less beautiful, featuring four outstanding lakes.

Not all of the hikes in this chapter are difficult. Wallace Falls State Park has a trio of big waterfalls. Woody Trail is a lush, quiet hike and a great choice for families. Some of the valley's biggest old-growth forest is found in this area. Deception Creek is a relaxed hike through an incredible forest of big timber beside a frolicking creek. And as for lakes, Snoqualmie Lake and Blanca Lake are ideal opportunities for families to head out for a picnic and a swim.

If the glint of sun hitting the surface of a distant lake is your idea of the perfect hiking destination, then Highway 2 is the right spot to begin your adventure.

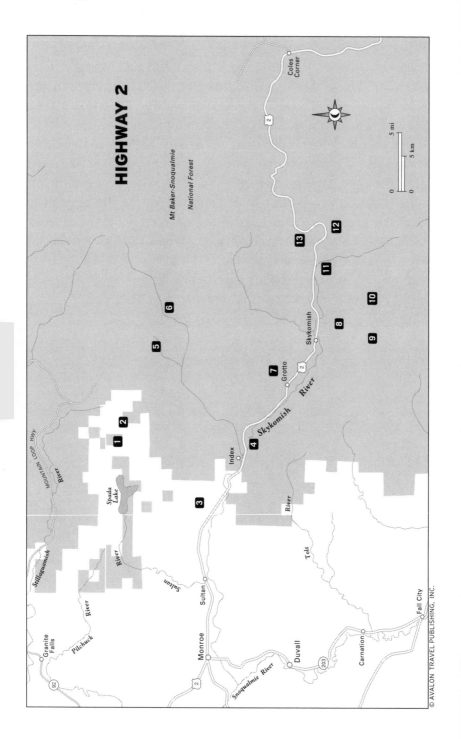

HIGHWAY 2

Mt Baker-Snoqualmie
National Forest

© AVALON TRAVEL PUBLISHING, INC.

Highway 2 Hikes

1 GREIDER LAKES

Greider Ridge Natural Resources Conservation Area

Level: Moderate

Hiking Time: 3 hours

Total Distance: 5.0 miles

Elevation Gain: 1,500 feet

Summary: A short but steep trail to a pair of low-elevation lakes in a rocky subalpine basin.

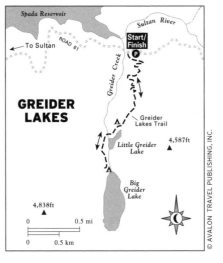

There is only one way to Greider Lakes: up. This hike may be short but it is strenuous. The trail relentlessly switchbacks up the steep hillside, quickly putting 1,500 feet of elevation between you and your car in just two miles. The hike has plenty of upsides, though. To take your mind off the exertion, the trail passes through some nice old-growth forest. The destination is Greider Lakes, a pair of low-elevation subalpine lakes, a rarity. Tucked away far off the main highway, this hike sees a fraction of the traffic that most other trails receive. If you've got rambunctious kids who need a good tiring-out, a hike to Greider Lakes is the ticket.

The Cascade Mountains are notoriously rainy, but this part of the range is especially wet, with up to 180 inches of precipitation a year. The extra rain and snow push the subalpine environment of mountain hemlocks and meadows down to Greider Lakes at 3,000 feet, an uncommon occurrence. Managed by Washington State Department of Resources, this area is designated Greider Ridge Natural Resources Conservation Area, our state's version of a wilderness designation.

From the trailhead, Greider Lakes Trail immediately passes Reflection Pond beside the parking lot (0.1 mile). Say goodbye to level trail as the hike begins the ascent to the lakes. Countless switchbacks ascend the steep hillside. The trail is often overtaken by rocks and roots—some built-in stair steps are high and difficult. Fortunately the route is shaded by impressive old-growth timber. As the trail approaches Little Greider

Steep rock walls frame Big Greider Lake.

Lake, the hillside is a precipitous drop to the right. The trail mercifully levels out and crosses the outlet of Little Greider Lake on an old, rickety bridge (2.0 miles)—watch your step! The trail then traverses a talus slope on the west side of Little Greider and drops slightly to Big Greider Lake (2.5 miles). Static Peak and the rocky cliffs of Greider Ridge frame the background of the lake.

Swimming, camping, and even fishing are popular activities at the lakes. There are several campsites and picnic spots at both lakes. The lakes have fish in their depths, but don't expect any big whoppers. The hike is best finished with a swim in Big Greider. In early summer, the bugs are bad at both lakes. Big Greider Lake is the best turnaround spot. The trail continues, however, past the outlet of Big Greider Lake, climbing sharply to a viewpoint at 3,600 feet (3.1 miles) and the end of the trail.

Directions
From Seattle, drive north on I-5 to Highway 2 in Everett. From Bellevue and the east side of Lake Washington, drive north on I-405 to Highway 522 in Bothell. Turn north on Highway 522 and drive to Highway 2 in Monroe.

From Monroe, drive east on Highway 2 to Sultan Basin Road, just after passing through the town of Sultan. Turn left and drive north on Sultan Basin Road. At 13 miles, stay right at the unsigned fork. At 14 miles, register your vehicle at the Department of Natural Resources visitor station (it's free) and stay to the right at the fork. At 19 miles, stay right at the unsigned fork. At 21 miles is Greider Lakes trailhead, on the right.

Information and Contact

This trail is accessible mid-May–October and is open to hikers and leashed dogs. Permits are not required. Parking and access are free. For topographic maps, ask Green Trails for No. 142, Index, or ask the USGS for Mount Stickney. For more information, contact Washington State Department of Natural Resources, P.O. Box 47001, Olympia, WA 98504, 360/902-1000.

2 BOULDER LAKE

Greider Ridge Natural Resources Conservation Area

Level: Easy/Moderate

Hiking Time: 4.5 hours

Total Distance: 7.6 miles

Elevation Gain: 2,000 feet

Summary: A wild and lightly maintained trail to a low-elevation subalpine lake without the crowds.

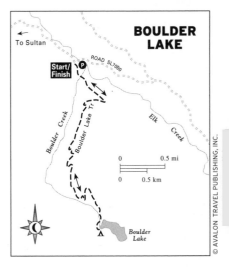

Tucked away in Sultan Basin, Boulder Lake is relatively unknown amongst the hiking masses. This hike is located on land managed by the Washington State Department of Natural Resources (DNR) and thus receives little attention compared to better-known hikes in the Mount Baker–Snoqualmie National Forest. So if solitude is your goal, this is the hike for you. The trail is rough and rarely maintained, adding to the wild feel. Boulder Lake is the highlight of the hike, nestled beneath rocky Greider Ridge.

Boulder Lake Trail delves into Greider Ridge Natural Resources Conservation Area, the state's version of a wilderness designation. The terrain is unscarred by logging and protects the unique low-elevation subalpine setting. Although wildernesses are better-known, Natural Resources Conservation Areas serve an important role for recreation and conservation. Unfortunately, the DNR is unable to provide adequate trail maintenance, and it is apparent on this hike.

Boulder Lake Trail begins on an old logging road and quickly crosses Boulder Creek on a large bridge as the stream cascades over exposed bedrock (0.2 mile). The trail climbs swiftly through the dense forest before reaching an exposed rockslide (1.2 miles). This section is rocky, often choked by overgrown brush, and a bit unpleasant. The trail eventually enters the forest on improved tread (1.8 miles). Grin and bear the less-than-scenic first half of the hike.

Boulder Lake Trail traverses the hillside with the occasional switchback as it climbs steadily but never steeply. The last mile of trail is the best. Old-growth trees begin to dominate the forest, and huckleberry bushes line the

a section of boardwalk through a wet meadow on Boulder Lake Trail

trail. Delightfully, the trail finally reaches Boulder Lake (3.8 miles). The lake basin is a mix of forest and meadows, with Greider Ridge lining the background. There are numerous campsites at the lake—camping is permitted June 15–October 15. Be forewarned that the lake can be extremely buggy but also makes a great swimming hole. Warm summer days call for bug juice and a swimsuit.

Directions

From Seattle, drive north on I-5 to Highway 2 in Everett. From Bellevue and the east side of Lake Washington, drive north on I-405 to Highway 522 in Bothell. Turn north on Highway 522 and drive to Highway 2 in Monroe.

From Monroe, drive east on Highway 2 to Sultan Basin Road, just after passing through the town of Sultan. Turn left and drive north on Sultan Basin Road. At 13 miles, stay right at the unsigned fork. At 14 miles, register your vehicle at the Department of Natural Resources visitor station (it's free) and stay to the right at the fork. At 19 miles, stay right at the unsigned fork. At 22 miles is Boulder Lake trailhead, on the right.

Information and Contact

This trail is accessible mid-May–October and is open to hikers and leashed dogs. Permits are not required. Parking and access are free. For topographic maps, ask Green Trails for No. 142, Index, or ask the USGS for Mount Stickney. For more information, contact Washington State Department of Natural Resources, P.O. Box 47001, Olympia, WA 98504, 360/902-1000.

3 WOODY TRAIL TO WALLACE FALLS   BEST 🌙
Wallace Falls State Park

🏔️ 🐴 👫

Level: Easy/Moderate

Hiking Time: 3 hours

Total Distance: 5.6 miles

Elevation Gain: 1,100 feet

Summary: An excellent forested trail along the Wallace River to the area's biggest waterfalls.

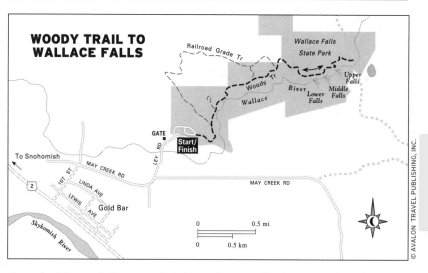

Great for hikers of all ages and abilities, there are few better trails within such easy reach of Seattle. Nestled within Wallace Falls State Park, one of Washington's best, Woody Trail makes an easy ramble along the Wallace River to Wallace Falls. Wallace Falls are some of the Cascades' best-known waterfalls, with more than nine drops of at least 50 feet. The tallest cascade, with a drop of 265 feet, is visible from Highway 2. But why just see something from the highway when you can check it out up close?

Woody Trail begins beneath towering power lines but soon ducks into the cool forest. Stay right at the first, well-signed junction (0.5 mile), and follow the trail as it parallels the cascading river. The rangers at the park do an excellent job maintaining the trail, in spite of the heavy traffic. Numerous structures, including several great bridges, help to keep feet dry. The trail gently climbs to a viewpoint at the Lower Falls (1.8 miles). Here, a picnic shelter awaits you for a hard-earned lunch. This section gains only 300 feet and is a great place to turn around for a shorter, easier hike.

Many small streams cross Woody Trail on the way to Wallace Falls.

A second viewpoint appears at Middle Falls (2.2 miles), not long after the shelter. Middle Falls are the largest of the cascades, creating a storm of spray in the heavy flow of springtime. Keep an eye on little ones and make sure dogs are leashed. Despite barriers around the edge, the park sees numerous accidents each year along the precipitous edges. From the middle viewpoint, the trail climbs up several switchbacks to a third viewpoint at the Upper Falls (2.8 miles). This is the steepest portion of the trail, where much of the effort is expended. The Upper Falls are worth visiting, though, if only to say that you've hiked the whole trail.

A great time to visit Wallace Falls is the fall, when the leaves of many hardwood trees lining the river create a palette of color. The trail often sees a little snow in winter, but it is always accessible. The busy season is summer, when Woody Trail gets more than its fair share of visitors. It's understandable why.

Directions

From Seattle, drive north on I-5 to Highway 2 in Everett. Drive east on Highway 2 to the town of Gold Bar. Turn left (north) on 1st Street and drive 0.5 mile to May Creek Road. Turn right and drive 1.5 miles to the park entrance. The well-signed trailhead is near the main parking area in the park.

Information and Contact

This trail is accessible year-round, except on Mondays and Tuesdays October–March, and is open to hikers and leashed dogs. A $5 day-use fee is required to park here and is payable at the trailhead, or you can get an annual State Parks Pass for $50; contact Washington State Parks and Recreation, 360/902-8500. For topographic maps, ask Green Trails for No. 142, Index, or ask the USGS for Gold Bar and Wallace Lake. For more information, contact Wallace Falls State Park, P.O. Box 230, Gold Bar, WA 98251, 360/793-0420.

4 LAKE SERENE TRAIL   BEST ☾
Mount Baker-Snoqualmie National Forest

🏕 🏊 ⛺ 👫

Level: Moderate   **Total Distance:** 7.2 miles

Hiking Time: 4.5 hours   **Elevation Gain:** 1,950 feet

Summary: A challenging haul to one of Washington's greatest low-elevation lakes.

Lake Serene Trail packs it all in. Starting just a stone's throw from Highway 2, the challenging route offers regular points of interest over its 3.6-mile course. First up are a pair of crossings at the bottom of scenic Bridal Veil Falls. As the trail climbs, it breaks out in the open and offers far-flung views of the Skykomish Valley. Finally, the trail reaches Lake Serene. Although it lies at just 2,500 feet of elevation, the lake takes on an alpine feel nestled beneath the towering cliffs of Mount Index. Certainly, Lake Serene is one of the valley's most beautiful lakes.

Lake Serene Trail is all business and rarely stops climbing. The first half of the trail is a steady incline through hardwood forests of red alder and big leaf maple. Several streams ramble across the trail but aren't big enough to soak the boots. The Forest Service has signed the trail as it crosses a decommissioned road (1.5 miles). Just beyond the road, the trail reaches Bridal Veil Falls Trail junction (1.6 miles)—stay left on Lake Serene Trail as it drops to a bridge crossing the creek, directly beneath a set of the large falls. In the spring, snowmelt feeds the creek until the falls are a roaring cascade.

Beyond Bridal Veil Creek, the trail makes an unbroken, vigorous climb in its latter half. Ducking into old-growth forest, this portion of the trail features many wooden structures. Numerous crib steps only add to the pain of the countless switchbacks. Frequently, the forest breaks and reveals great views of the valley below. This section of the trail will challenge some hikers and is a little too much for children, but Lake Serene is within reach. Regular breaks will recharge worn-out hikers.

In return for the hard work, the trail reaches the large bowl holding Lake Serene (3.6 miles). Mount Index towers more than 3,000 feet above the lake, providing a dramatic setting. On hot summer days, Lake Serene is the perfect swimming hole. Across the bridge spanning the lake's outlet, a pair of signed side trails visit first, a viewpoint of the valley and second, Lunch Rock. Aptly named, Lunch Rock is an enormous slab of glacially smoothed bedrock. Few afternoons are better-spent than basking in the sun here.

On the way to Lake Serene, you can see Mount Index poking through the clouds.

Options

Bridal Veil Falls Trail is a steep 0.5-mile climb to an excellent viewpoint at the middle falls, which are the largest. For those with the energy, it's a good side trip on the way down. The junction is 1.6 miles up Lake Serene Trail, before it crosses Bridal Veil Creek—turn right to reach the viewpoint.

Directions

From Seattle, drive north on I-5 to Everett and turn east on Highway 2 to Mount Index Road, just beyond milepost 35. Turn right and drive 0.2 mile to a very short access road, on the right, and the signed trailhead.

Information and Contact

This trail is usually accessible May–October and is open to hikers and leashed dogs. There is no wheelchair access. A federal Northwest Forest Pass is required to park here. For a map of Mount Baker–Snoqualmie National Forest, contact the Outdoor Recreation Information Center at the downtown Seattle REI. For topographic maps, ask Green Trails for No. 142, Index, or ask the USGS for Index. For more information, contact Mount Baker–Snoqualmie National Forest, Skykomish Ranger Station, 74920 Northeast Stevens Pass Highway, Skykomish, WA 98288, 360/677-2414.

⑤ BLANCA LAKE   BEST █

in the Henry M. Jackson Wilderness of Mount Baker-Snoqualmie
National Forest

Level: Strenuous

Total Distance: 7.2 miles

Hiking Time: 6 hours

Elevation Gain: 3,300 feet

Summary: A strenuous hike through great old-growth forest to small Virgin Lake at the pass and down to spectacular Blanca Lake.

Blanca Lake is no free lunch. This hike's final destination is incredibly beautiful, with emerald green waters surrounded by high cliffs. To the north, the rocky peaks of Monte Cristo and Kyes Peaks stand above Columbia Glacier and a series of waterfalls. Blanca Lake certainly does not disappoint in the scenery department. The hike itself, however, is a different story, where elevation change is the name of the game. The trail steeply climbs 2,700 feet in three miles before cruelly dropping 600 feet on rugged tread to Blanca Lake. This hike will have even the fittest of hikers working up a good sweat.

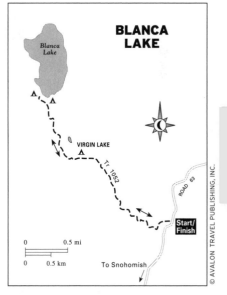

Blanca Lake Trail wastes little time before beginning the grinding climb. For three miles, the trail ruthlessly switchbacks up the backside of Troublesome Mountain. Although taxing, the trail rises through a great forest of old-growth hemlock, fir, and cedar. Granddaddy trees will regularly catch your attention. Huckleberry bushes are also prolific along the trail—August is peak berry time.

Blanca Lake Trail reaches the crest of the ridge in a parkland of meadows (3.0 miles) with views of the Cascade Crest through the trees to the west. In a small saddle on the immediate other side of the crest lies Virgin Lake amongst the trees (3.1 miles). Many hikers have lunch here and call it a day. That may not be a bad idea because the hike gets even tougher from here. Trail snacks and water will be quickly gobbled up along this hike, so packing extra portions of each will be much appreciated.

© SCOTT LEONARD

an old, burned-out cedar on the trail to
Blanca Lake

From Virgin Lake, the trail drops steeply to Blanca Lake. The tread is strewn with rocks and roots; this section is difficult on the way up and treacherous on the way down. The rough hike is rewarded finally with Blanca Lake in its serene setting, where Keyes Peak towers above Columbia Glacier. There are several campsites located at the outlet of the lake. Stick to the main trail at all times—the meadows here are fragile and have seen much past abuse. In spite of the difficult hike, Blanca Lake sees many visitors.

Directions

From Seattle, drive north on I-5 to Highway 2 in Everett. From Bellevue and the east side of Lake Washington, drive north on I-405 to Highway 522 in Bothell. Turn north on Highway 522 and drive to Highway 2 in Monroe.

From Monroe, drive east on Highway 2 to North Fork Road (just past milepost 35), signed for the town of Index. Turn left and drive northeast on North Fork Road. At one mile, continue straight ahead on North Fork Road, which becomes Road 63. At 14 miles, stay left at the fork on Road 63. At 15 miles, turn left on Forest Service Road 6300. Drive two miles to Blanca Lake trailhead.

Information and Contact

This trail is accessible mid-June–October and is open to hikers and leashed dogs. A federal Northwest Forest Pass is required to park here. For a map of Mount Baker–Snoqualmie National Forest, contact the Outdoor Recreation Information Center at the downtown Seattle REI. For topographic maps, ask Green Trails for No. 143, Monte Cristo, or ask the USGS for Blanca Lake. For more information, contact Mount Baker–Snoqualmie National Forest, Skykomish Ranger Station, 74920 Northeast Stevens Pass Highway, Skykomish, WA 98288, 360/677-2414.

6 WEST CADY RIDGE   BEST ◖

in the Henry M. Jackson Wilderness of Mount Baker-Snoqualmie
National Forest

🏠 🔭 🦌 🐴 ⛷

Level: Moderate   **Total Distance:** 7.6 miles

Hiking Time: 4.5 hours   **Elevation Gain:** 2,300 feet

Summary: A steady climb through old-growth forest to parkland meadows
and great views of the Cascade Crest.

Deep in the heart of the Henry M.
Jackson Wilderness, this is one of this
book's most remote trails. The hike
climbs steadily through old forest to
the crest of West Cady Ridge, blessed
with miles of big-sky meadows. Naturally, the views are impressive. It's a
two-hour drive from Seattle to the
trailhead—the trail's distant location
helps keep the crowds at bay. This is a
favorite with horse riders, who combine West Cady Ridge with several
other nearby trails as part of a long
loop through the wilderness. Don't

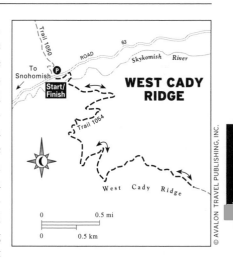

expect an easy time when seeking out such grand scenery—the trail is hot and
dry in the middle of summer.

Within minutes of leaving the trailhead, West Cady Ridge Trail crosses
the North Fork Skykomish River on a large wooden bridge (0.1 mile). This is
a great place for a crossing, where the river pours through a narrow gorge in
the granite bedrock. From here, the trail climbs up the hillside at a moderate
grade. The forest is classic Cascade old growth, with enormous Douglas firs,
western hemlocks, and western red cedars providing welcome shade.

Despite the horse traffic, the tread is in very good condition. Occasional wet
patches are spanned by old cedar boardwalks. The trail crosses several small
streams in the first 1.5 miles, but beyond that it is bone dry. Be sure to carry
lots of water, especially if hiking with a dog. After reaching a small saddle
between the ridge and Excelsior Mountain (2.0 miles), the trail switchbacks
up the hillside at a steeper rate. The forest breaks into wide open views (2.5
miles) and reaches a small summit on the ridge (3.8 miles) before dropping

down along the ridge. This small summit is a good stopping point for this hike—the views are as good as any you could ask for. Keyes, Monte Cristo, and Sloan Peaks line the western horizon while Glacier Peak stands out to the north. August is peak berry season for the hordes of huckleberry bushes that line the entire route.

Options

Extending this hike into a longer trip is easy. West Cady Ridge Trail rambles through parkland meadows for the length of the ridge to Benchmark Mountain (7.2 miles one-way) and eventually connects to the Pacific Crest Trail (8.7 miles). From the viewpoint on the first summit, described above, West Cady Ridge sticks to the crest of the ridge and enjoys nonstop views. The summit of Benchmark Mountain reveals more mountains to the east. Extra water and sunscreen are especially important on this longer option.

Directions

From Seattle, drive north on I-5 to Highway 2 in Everett. From Bellevue and the east side of Lake Washington, drive north on I-405 to Highway 522 in Bothell. Turn north on Highway 522 and drive to Highway 2 in Monroe.

From Monroe, drive east on Highway 2 to North Fork Road (just past milepost 35), signed for the town of Index. Turn left and drive northeast on

West Cady Ridge is awash in spectacular views of Glacier Peak and the Cascade Crest.

© SCOTT LEONARD

North Fork Road. At one mile, continue straight ahead on North Fork Road, which becomes Road 63. At 14 miles, where the pavement ends, turn left at the fork and continue on Road 63. At 16 miles, stay to the right on Road 63. At 18.5 miles, the road ends at a parking area for a trio of trailheads. West Cady Ridge is signed on the right side of the graveled parking area.

Information and Contact

This trail is accessible July–October and is open to hikers, leashed dogs, and horses. A federal Northwest Forest Pass is required to park here. For a map of Mount Baker–Snoqualmie National Forest, contact the Outdoor Recreation Information Center at the downtown Seattle REI. For topographic maps, ask Green Trails for No. 143, Monte Cristo, and No. 144, Benchmark Mountain, or ask the USGS for Blanca Lake and Benchmark Mountain. For more information, contact Mount Baker–Snoqualmie National Forest, Skykomish Ranger Station, 74920 Northeast Stevens Pass Highway, Skykomish, WA 98288, 360/677-2414.

7 BARCLAY LAKE
Mount Baker-Snoqualmie National Forest

Level: Easy

Hiking Time: 2 hours

Total Distance: 4.2 miles

Elevation Gain: 250 feet

Summary: A great hike for the whole family through lush green forest to Barclay Lake below the sheer wall of Baring Mountain.

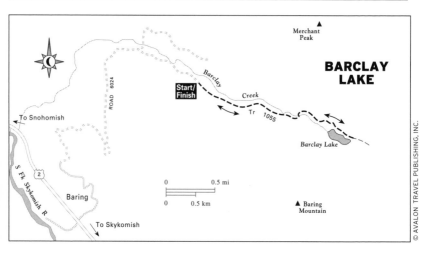

The hike to Barclay Lake is one of the most family-friendly trips along Highway 2. The hike is an easy stroll through a lush forest of fir trees and ferns. The rock wall of Baring Mountain towers 3,700 feet over the water. Following Barclay Creek to its source, the trail gains an unnoticeable 250 feet in two miles—even the smallest of hikers will dig this walk. Barclay Lake is a good idea in the fall and spring, when other trails are still snowbound. The trail's low elevation (2,422 feet) means it's snow-free by early spring. Winter usually brings several feet of snow on the trail, so this is also an easy and fun snowshoe hike.

The hike to the lake is straightforward with no confusing junctions. Barclay Lake Trail leaves the parking lot and enters a tunnel of dense forest. It's not long before the forest improves, opening up to some big trees and lush undergrowth. The tread is wide and smooth with a few rough spots here and there. The trail has been improved considerably in recent years, with long stretches of boardwalk in sections once notoriously muddy. Watch your step in the rain—these boardwalks can be slippery.

Barclay Lake Trail crosses the creek on a log footbridge (1.6 miles) and quickly arrives at Barclay Lake (2.0 miles). The trail runs along the northern lakeshore. There are a pair of large picnic areas (2.0 miles and 2.1 miles) that mark the end of the hike. The lake is an inviting swimming and fishing spot on hot summer days, so be sure to pack swim trunks and fishing poles. As for views, the imposing tower of Baring Mountain shoots into the sky on the south side of the lake. To the north but difficult to see are Gunn and Merchant Peaks. Both sides of the valley surrounding the trail and lake are part of the proposed Wild Sky Wilderness, currently muddled up in Congress.

Directions

From Seattle, drive north on I-5 to Highway 2 in Everett. From Bellevue and the east side of Lake Washington, drive north on I-405 to Highway 522 in Bothell. Turn north on Highway 522 and drive to Highway 2 in Monroe.

From Monroe, drive east on Highway 2. After passing milepost 41, turn left (north) on Forest Service Road 6024. Cross the railroad tracks and drive 4.5 miles to the signed trailhead at the end of the road.

Information and Contact

This trail is accessible April–November and is open to hikers and leashed dogs. A federal Northwest Forest Pass is required to park here. For a map of Mount Baker–Snoqualmie National Forest, contact the Outdoor Recreation Information Center at the downtown Seattle REI. For topographic maps, ask Green Trails for No. 143, Monte Cristo, or ask the USGS for Baring. For more information, contact Mount Baker–Snoqualmie National Forest, Skykomish Ranger Station, 74920 Northeast Stevens Pass Highway, Skykomish, WA 98288, 360/677-2414.

8 NECKLACE VALLEY

in the Alpine Lakes Wilderness of Mount Baker-Snoqualmie
National Forest

Level: Strenuous   **Total Distance:** 16.4 miles

Hiking Time: 10 hours   **Elevation Gain:** 3,300 feet

Summary: A long, sometimes challenging hike to numerous high lakes in one of Washington's most esteemed lake basins.

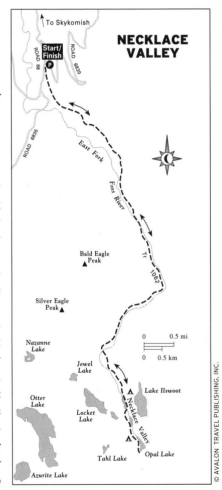

It's a long, hard hike into Necklace Valley. After five miles of river valley, the trail climbs 2,500 feet in a little more than two miles. Not exactly the stuff for beginners. For those who endure the challenge of reaching Necklace Valley, however, ample compensation awaits. Necklace Valley is home to a string of handsome lakes dotting a narrow, high valley. On nearly all sides are sheer cliffs, rocky slopes, and towering peaks, where patches of snow linger late into summer. The upper valley is wide open and filled with meadowy parkland, leaving lots of room to explore. This is a classic hike of the Alpine Lakes Wilderness.

The long length of the hike to Necklace Valley makes it a difficult day hike. Be prepared for a full day on the trail—the 16 miles of trail can easily take 10 hours. An early start helps—in case you're still hiking as daylight fades, an extra layer of clothing and a headlamp are worth their extra weight in the day pack. Plenty of trail food and extra water are also important items. If the length of this trek seems too much to fit into a day, this hike is a great candidate for an overnight backpacking trip. There are many established campsites located in the basin—the best are found along the shores of any lake.

Necklace Valley naturally draws comparisons to its western neighbor Foss Lakes. The trail to Necklace Valley is longer, a little less traveled, and the tread is more rugged. It visits smaller lakes but is every bit as scenic. From the trailhead, Necklace Valley Trail soon enters the wilderness (1.5 miles) and enjoys three miles of old-growth forest along the East Fork Foss River. This section of trail is easy and makes for a great hike by itself, especially in the late fall and early spring. Families will particularly enjoy this section.

The trail crosses glacial-fed East Fork Foss River on a bridge (4.8 miles) and gets down to business as the trail shoots up through the forest quickly and mercilessly. This section of trail is strewn with rocks and roots. The grade finally levels out after the trail shoots through the narrow entrance to Necklace Valley and discovers Jade Lake (7.6 miles). The trail skirts the shores of Emerald Lake (7.9 miles) and officially ends at Opal Lake (8.2 miles). Small trails lead to the numerous other lakes in the valley—getting lost is not difficult, so bringing a map is advised.

Directions

From Seattle, drive north on I-5 to Highway 2 in Everett. From Bellevue and the east side of Lake Washington, drive north on I-405 to Highway 522 in Bothell. Turn north on Highway 522 and drive to Highway 2 in Monroe.

From Monroe, drive east on Highway 2 to Foss River Road (Forest Service Road 68), shortly after passing the Skykomish Ranger Station. Turn right (south) onto Foss River Road. At 3.5 miles, stay right at the fork on Forest Service Road 68. At 4.5 miles, turn left into the unsigned parking lot and trailhead, immediately off the main road.

Information and Contact

This trail is accessible July–October and is open to hikers and leashed dogs. A federal Northwest Forest Pass is required to park here. For a map of Mount Baker–Snoqualmie National Forest, contact the Outdoor Recreation Information Center at the downtown Seattle REI. For topographic maps, ask Green Trails for No. 175, Skykomish, and No. 176, Stevens Pass, or ask the USGS for Skykomish, Big Snow Mountain, and Mount Daniel. For more information, contact Mount Baker–Snoqualmie National Forest, Skykomish Ranger Station, 74920 Northeast Stevens Pass Highway, Skykomish, WA 98288, 360/677-2414.

9 SNOQUALMIE LAKE

in the Alpine Lakes Wilderness of Mount Baker-Snoqualmie
National Forest

Level: Easy/Moderate

Total Distance: 14.0 miles

Hiking Time: 8 hours

Elevation Gain: 2,200 feet

Summary: An easy and customizable hike to four great lakes tucked away in the Alpine Lakes Wilderness.

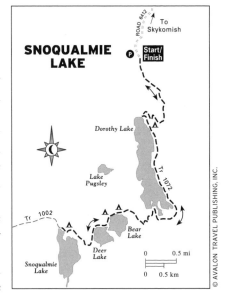

This long hike into the western end of Alpine Lakes Wilderness can easily be made shorter. The hike passes four lakes as it rambles through subalpine forests. Dorothy Lake is an easy two miles, Bear and Deer Lakes are a more moderate 5.5 miles, while Snoqualmie Lake is seven miles from the trailhead. This is a popular hike with families since there's lots to explore here with a chance for hikers of all abilities to experience it.

Snoqualmie and Dorothy Lake Trails make a long, east–west journey through the Alpine Lakes Wilderness, progressing from the Miller River in the Skykomish drainage over to the Taylor River in the Snoqualmie drainage. This recommended route begins off Highway 2 and is the shorter access to Snoqualmie Lake. It also features better trail and more virgin forest along the way. Although Dorothy Lake can feel crowded on summer weekends, the traffic on the trail from Dorothy Lake to Snoqualmie Lake thins considerably.

From the trailhead, Dorothy Lake Trail quickly begins the gradual ascent toward Dorothy Lake. The trail crosses the wilderness boundary and a sturdy wooden bridge over Camp Robber Creek (1.0 mile). The grade is a steady incline but is not difficult—800 feet gain in two miles to the northern end of Dorothy Lake (2.0 miles). Dorothy Lake is enormous and is dotted by small islands with forest covering the surrounding hillsides. Dorothy Lake is the first good turnaround point for those seeking a shorter hike.

Dorothy Lake Trail runs along the eastern shoreline and makes a sudden ascent to a pass (5.0 miles), the divider between the Snoqualmie and Skykomish watersheds. The trail becomes Snoqualmie Lake Trail at the pass and next skirts the shores of Bear and Deer Lakes (5.5 miles), separated by a small strip of land. Views up to Big Snow Mountain and other rocky ridges are great. The trail drops 600 feet to large Snoqualmie Lake (7.0 miles). Each of the lakes are popular fishing and swimming holes.

Options

The length of the hike to Snoqualmie Lake lends itself well to an overnight backpack. There are numerous campsites at all four lakes. On summer weekends, they tend to go quickly. Be sure to practice Leave No Trace camping.

Directions

From Seattle, drive north on I-5 to Highway 2 in Everett. From Bellevue and the eastside of Lake Washington, drive north on I-405 to Highway 522 in Bothell. Turn north on Highway 522 and drive to Highway 2 in Monroe.

From Monroe, drive east on Highway 2 to Money Creek Campground, three miles before the town of Skykomish. Turn right (south) onto the Old Cascade Highway. The road is just west of the highway tunnel. Drive the Old Cascade Highway for one mile, then turn right (south) onto the Miller River Road (Forest Service Road 6410). Continue on Forest Service Road 6412 for 9.5 miles to the road's end at the trailhead.

Information and Contact

This hike is accessible June–October and is open to hikers and leashed dogs. A federal Northwest Forest Pass is required to park here. For a map of Mount Baker–Snoqualmie National Forest, contact the Outdoor Recreation Information Center at the downtown Seattle REI. For topographic maps, ask Green Trails for No. 175, Skykomish, or ask the USGS for Snoqualmie Lake and Big Snow Mountain. For more information, contact Mount Baker–Snoqualmie National Forest, Skykomish Ranger Station, 74920 Northeast Stevens Pass Highway, Skykomish, WA 98288, 360/677-2414.

10 FOSS LAKES   BEST ◖

in the Alpine Lakes Wilderness of Mount Baker-Snoqualmie
National Forest

Level: Moderate/Strenuous   **Total Distance:** 13.6 miles

Hiking Time: 8 hours   **Elevation Gain:** 3,500 feet

Summary: A popular but lengthy hike to subalpine scenery along the shores
of five stunning lakes.

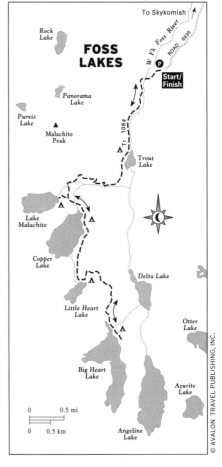

Foss Lakes is a classic hike in the Alpine Lake Wilderness. From low-elevation forests to high lakes, this is a perfect sampler of Seattle's favorite wilderness. The name of the hike might be a little misleading—there is no Foss Lake. Instead, the hike visits a series of scenic lakes that drain into the West Fork Foss River. After an easy walk in the woods to Trout Lake, the trail climbs to high-country beauties Lake Malachite, Copper Lake, Little Heart Lake, and Big Heart Lake. These are dramatic settings—rocky cliffs plunge into the high lakes' deep blue waters. And as far as swimming holes go, these were made for hot summer days. If this hike sounds great, that's because it is.

To Big Heart Lake and back is nearly 14 miles—for some, this is a long day of hiking. The many lakes along the way, however, provide plenty of opportunities to cut the trip short and still enjoy a beautiful day. Regardless of your final destination, extra water and snacks on this trip are greatly appreciated when the stomach begins to growl. The length of the hike makes it a very popular backpacking trip. There is camping at each of the lakes, although it goes quickly during the summer season. Finally, such easily accessible beauty is rarely left alone. As one of Highway 2's most popular hikes, this trail sees a lot of use, even bordering on abuse. Expect company on the trail and take care to avoid the many hiker-made footpaths.

West Fork Foss Trail begins easily, with little elevation gain along the first 1.5 miles to Trout Lake. Along the way, the trail passes one of the biggest Douglas firs you'll ever see. Only the largest of families will be able to wrap their arms around this one. Surrounded by forest, Trout Lake whets the appetite for the open subalpine lakes to come. This is a fine fishing hole and also a good turnaround for less serious hikers.

From Trout Lake, West Fork Foss Trail becomes demanding and works its way up to the lake basins. The trail climbs steeply, cruising in and out of forest alongside a beautiful cascading stream that offers needed refreshment on hot days. This is the trail's big climb, gaining 1,800 feet in two miles. As the toughest incline fades away, the junction to Lake Malachite appears (3.5 miles). Hang a right for a short, optional detour to the hike's second lake.

From the junction, West Fork Foss Trail continues via the left fork and quickly reaches Copper Lake (3.8 miles) and Little Heart Lake (5.0 miles). Ringed by rocky cliffs and talus slopes, the lakes are some of the most scenic in the Alpine Lakes Wilderness. This stretch of trail is the nicest of the hike—a level grade in subalpine forest from lake to lake. The crowds also thin considerably beyond Copper Lake. Big Heart Lake, the hike's final destination, requires a bit more work. The trail climbs to the hike's high point (4,900 feet) before losing some of its elevation to reach the shores of Big Heart Lake (6.8 miles), the largest and most striking of the lakes.

Directions

From Seattle, drive north on I-5 to Highway 2 in Everett. From Bellevue and the east side of Lake Washington, drive north on I-405 to Highway 522 in Bothell. Turn north on Highway 522 and drive to Highway 2 in Monroe.

From Monroe, drive east on Highway 2 to Foss River Road (Forest Service Road 68), just after passing the Skykomish Ranger Station. Turn right (south) onto Foss River Road. At 3.5 miles, stay right at the fork in the road on Forest Service Road 68. At five miles, turn left on signed Forest Service Road 6835. At seven miles is the signed parking area and trailhead at the end of the road.

Information and Contact

This trail is accessible June–October and is open to hikers and leashed dogs. A federal Northwest Forest Pass is required to park here. For a map of Mount

Baker–Snoqualmie National Forest, contact the Outdoor Recreation Information Center at the downtown Seattle REI. For topographic maps, ask Green Trails for No. 175, Skykomish, or ask the USGS for Big Snow Mountain and Skykomish. For more information, contact Mount Baker–Snoqualmie National Forest, Skykomish Ranger Station, 74920 Northeast Stevens Pass Highway, Skykomish, WA 98288, 360/677-2414.

11 DECEPTION CREEK

in the Alpine Lakes Wilderness of Mount Baker-Snoqualmie
National Forest

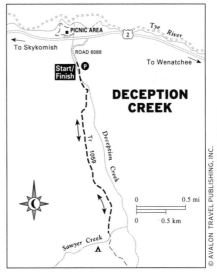

Level: Easy/Moderate

Hiking Time: 2.5 hours

Total Distance: 4.2 miles

Elevation Gain: 900 feet

Summary: A superb valley hike beside rumbling Deception Creek through prime old-growth forest.

Some trips into the wilderness need not culminate at a vista or high alpine lake. Sometimes, simple travel within giant forests and along a cool, murmuring creek is the end in itself. That is certainly the case with Deception Creek, a great stroll through shady, cool Cascade forest with access to high-country lakes. This is one of our region's best wilderness hikes through old-growth forest. This route ends at a campsite two miles from the trailhead, but if the mood strikes you, you can just keep wandering up the valley.

Deception Creek Trail begins on the northern shores of the stream and quickly enters the wilderness (0.2 mile). The first impressive stream crossing happens soon thereafter, where the trail crosses Deception Creek (0.5 mile) on an enormous downed tree supplemented with much-needed hand railings. Already the hike is a success, as this is a beautiful section of Deception Creek cascading over waterfalls beside big trees.

Deception Creek Trail now features a bit of up and down grade as it slowly climbs up the valley. This is Cascadia at its best, with the forest full of large Douglas firs, western red cedars, and western hemlocks. Moss grows on most everything while the forest floor becomes a carpet of ferns at times. The recommended turnaround point is when Deception Creek Trail crosses Sawyer Creek on a wooden bridge (2.1 miles). Several campsites are found on the far side of the stream and make a great picnic site.

Options

If you feel like hiking farther, Deception Creek Trail will accommodate. It eventually leaves the valley floor to ascend the valley wall. A connector trail (on the left at 7.3 miles) leads up to the Pacific Crest Trail and Deception Lakes (8.3 miles), the hike's best lake option.

Directions

From Seattle, drive north on I-5 to Highway 2 in Everett. From Bellevue and the eastside of Lake Washington, drive north on I-405 to Highway 522 in Bothell. Turn north on Highway 522 and drive to Highway 2 in Monroe. From Monroe, drive east on Highway 2 to Forest Service Road 6088, immediately beyond Deception Falls picnic area. Turn right and drive 0.3 mile to the well-signed trailhead beneath the power lines.

Information and Contact

This trail is accessible April–November and is open to hikers and dogs. A federal Northwest Forest Pass is required to park here. For a map of Mount Baker–Snoqualmie National Forest, contact the Outdoor Recreation Information Center at the downtown Seattle REI. For topographic maps, ask Green Trails for No. 176, Stevens Pass, or ask the USGS for Scenic. For more information, contact Mount Baker–Snoqualmie National Forest, Skykomish Ranger Station, 74920 Northeast Stevens Pass Highway, Skykomish, WA 98288, 360/677-2414.

12 SURPRISE LAKE

in the Alpine Lakes Wilderness of Mount Baker-Snoqualmie
National Forest

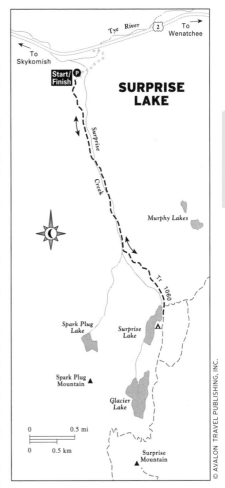

Level: Moderate   **Total Distance:** 8.0 miles

Hiking Time: 4 hours   **Elevation Gain:** 2,300 feet

Summary: This popular hike makes a steady, moderate climb to a scenic lake surrounded by rocky mountains.

Railroad tracks, buzzing power lines, and a gaggle of cars parked at the trailhead suggest Surprise Lake may be anything but a great hike. First impressions aren't always what they're cracked up to be, and that is the first pleasant surprise of this hike. The trail to Surprise Lake is in fact a scenic but heavily traveled route, climbing beside a rumbling creek to its headwaters. This is a classic hike in the Alpine Lakes Wilderness, offering a refreshing swim amidst high-country meadows and rocky peaks. This hike is easily extended—a pair of options climb to lonely Glacier Lake or vistas at Pieper Pass.

Surprise Creek Trail begins on the exposed logging road leading south from the trailhead but quickly says good-bye to civilization and enters old-growth forest (0.2 mile). The lake may be the destination, but Surprise Creek is the highlight of the hike. The trail spends its first three miles paralleling the clear creek as it spills over numerous waterfalls and cascades. The trail crosses Surprise Creek on a foot log (1.1 miles) in addition to other smaller streams.

SURPRISE
LAKE

To Skykomish

Start/Finish

Tye River → To Wenatchee

Surprise Creek

Murphy Lakes

Tr. 1060

Spark Plug Lake

Surprise Lake

Spark Plug Mountain ▲

Glacier Lake

0   0.5 mi
0   0.5 km

Surprise Mountain ▲

© AVALON TRAVEL PUBLISHING, INC.

The moderate grade steepens as it makes the final climb up the valley headwall (2.5 miles). This is the toughest section of the hike, gaining 1,200 feet in just 1.5 miles. The ascent finally levels out, the trail breaks out of the forest, and—surprise—you find yourself on the shores of Surprise Lake (4.0 miles). Rocky slopes rise to views of several peaks, including Spark Plug and Thunder Mountain. Many small places for a picnic can be found around the lake. Bring your swimming suit or just wear your birthday suit—this is an ideal swimming hole.

Options

Surprise Creek Trail doesn't end at the lake—it continues up to the Pacific Crest Trail and a pair of good destinations. From the shore of Surprise Lake, Surprise Lake Trail continues up the small ridge in the middle of the lake basin to a junction with the PCT (4.7 miles). Stay right on the PCT as it climbs above Glacier Lake (5.1 miles). Several obvious footpaths lead down to the lakeshore. Or continue south on the PCT as it climbs up to 5,900-foot Pieper Pass (6.6 miles). The meadowy pass offers views of the large glaciers on Mount Hinman and Mount Daniel. There is a lot of high country to explore around here and likely more than a few extra surprises.

Directions

From Seattle, drive north on I-5 to Highway 2 in Everett. From Bellevue and the east side of Lake Washington, drive north on I-405 to Highway 522 in Bothell. Turn north on Highway 522 and drive to Highway 2 in Monroe.

From Monroe, drive east on Highway 2. A half mile past milepost 58 is an unsigned road on the right. Turn right and follow the road as it enters a wide, open servicing center for Burlington-Northern Railroad. Cross the two sets of railroad tracks and turn right onto a spur road on the far right, paralleling the tracks. Continue 0.2 mile to the signed trailhead at road's end.

Information and Contact

This trail is accessible July–October and is open to hikers and leashed dogs. A federal Northwest Forest Pass is required to park here. For a map of Mount Baker–Snoqualmie National Forest, contact the Outdoor Recreation Information Center at the downtown Seattle REI. For topographic maps, ask Green Trails for No. 176, Stevens Pass, or ask the USGS for Scenic. For more information, contact Mount Baker–Snoqualmie National Forest, Skykomish Ranger Station, 74920 Northeast Stevens Pass Highway, Skykomish, WA 98288, 360/677-2414.

13 LAKE VALHALLA

in the Henry M. Jackson Wilderness of Mount Baker-Snoqualmie
National Forest

Level: Easy/Moderate

Total Distance: 10.6 miles

Hiking Time: 6 hours

Elevation Gain: 1,500 feet

Summary: A popular trip on the Pacific Crest Trail north of Stevens Pass to Lake Valhalla.

This is an easy hike along the famed Pacific Crest Trail. Walking north from Stevens Pass, the PCT makes use of an old roadbed before entering the wilderness and climbing to Lake Valhalla. The PCT is a goliath in American hiking legend, running 2,600 miles through the Sierras and Cascades from Mexico to Canada, so naturally, this is a popular hike. A trailhead right on Highway 2 and an easy grade add to the hike's appeal. This is a good hike for kids and infrequent hikers.

From the trailhead at Stevens Pass, the PCT runs along an old logging road. The tread is wide and flat—the trail gradually drops several hundred feet over the first two miles. This stretch of trail is mostly open, providing good views to the neighboring ridges. The PCT crosses a small creek and begins gently climbing (2.1 miles). The trail enters the wilderness (2.3 miles) and passes through a pair of small basins (3.0 miles and 3.5 miles).

The PCT now begins the final climb to Lake Valhalla. The tread gets a bit rough in spots as the trail switchbacks quickly up the hillside. This is the toughest section of the trail, but it gains just 1,200 in two miles. After reaching a crest (5.0 miles), Lake Valhalla is in full sight. Continue on the PCT to a junction located in a meadow above the lake (5.1 miles)—turn right to drop to the lakeshore (5.3 miles). A fishing pole and swim trunks are good things to bring along. The basin is a large glacial cirque beneath Lichtenberg Mountain and sports good views to the south.

Directions

From Seattle, drive north on I-5 to Highway 2 in Everett. From Bellevue and the east side of Lake Washington, drive north on I-405 to Highway 522 in Bothell. Turn north on Highway 522 and drive to Highway 2 in Monroe.

From Monroe, drive east on Highway 2 to Stevens Pass. On the left (west) side of the highway is a large parking lot. The signed trailhead for the Pacific Crest Trail is in the back of the parking lot and to the right of several cabins.

Information and Contact

This trail is accessible mid-June–October and is open to hikers and leashed dogs. A federal Northwest Forest Pass is required to park here. For a map of Mount Baker–Snoqualmie National Forest, contact the Outdoor Recreation Information Center at the downtown Seattle REI. For topographic maps, ask Green Trails for No. 175, Skykomish, or ask the USGS for Labyrinth Mountain. For more information, contact Mount Baker–Snoqualmie National Forest, Skykomish Ranger Station, 74920 Northeast Stevens Pass Highway, Skykomish, WA 98288, 360/677-2414.

INTERSTATE 90

© SCOTT LEONARD

BEST HIKES

Seattle's backyard, the North Fork Snoqualmie River

Valley, is the chosen route for Interstate 90, one of the few interstates in America to be designated a National Scenic Highway. The valley is a popular corridor for outdoor recreation, largely due to the fact that the Middle Fork Snoqualmie is the biggest valley close to Seattle and that Interstate 90 provides quick and convenient access. Plenty of hiking diversity can be found in this region, with picturesque waterfalls and lakes as common features. Many of these hikes climb up to summits or subalpine parklands and are excellent options for a quick trip to the wilderness.

The river and valley split east of the town of North Bend. Interstate 90 travels up the South Fork of the Snoqualmie River, but several great hikes diverge off to the Middle Fork Snoqualmie River. Middle Fork Trail offers an easy river ramble that is great for families. Hikes to Hester Lake and Myrtle Lake share the quiet trail up Dingford Creek before splitting off to separate high country lakes.

The lake hikes in the valley are among the most popular anywhere in the state. Denny Creek Trail passes a pair of big waterfalls before reaching beautiful Lake Melakwa. Snow and Rachel Lakes are two outstanding subalpine lakes, typical of this valley. Adventures to Lake

Annette, Lake Lillian, and Margaret Lake all offer stunning scenery and an unforgettable experience.

Bandera and Granite Mountains are two of the more challenging hikes highlighted in this book – both yield staggering views of the Cascades. Mount Si is Washington's busiest trail: The legendary peak is packed with hikers nearly year-round. The most beautiful hike, though, follows the Pacific Crest Trail to Kendall Katwalk, a narrow walkway atop a vertical granite cliff with picturesque lakes along the way.

Of course, the valley offers a few family favorites, too. Little Si, a smaller version of Mount Si, offers sweeping views of the valley and is easy enough to give older children a real feeling of accomplishment. Talapus Lake is a good hike for families, as well, passing through a nice fir forest before reaching the scenic lake. Rattlesnake Mountain takes hikers to its rock ledge, jutting out into thin air and offering a great view of the Cascades. And Twin Falls, leading to a pair of big waterfalls on the North Fork Snoqualmie, is perfect for all ages.

With so much treasure in one valley, it's no wonder that this area attracts so much attention – hiking in this region is a recommended trip no matter what the season.

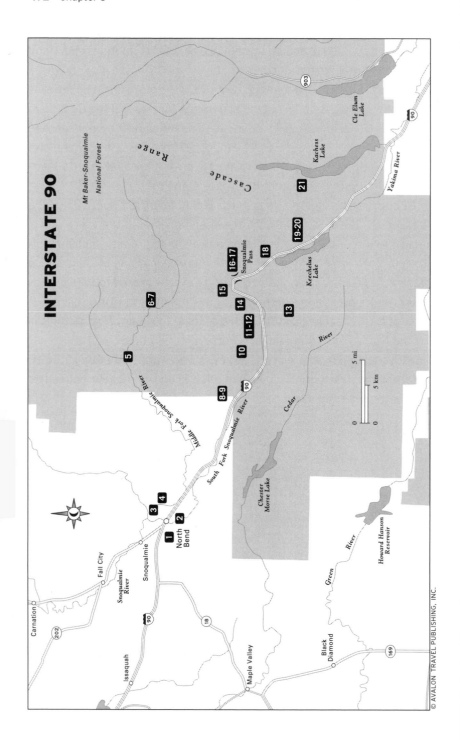

INTERSTATE 90

Interstate 90 Hikes

1 RATTLESNAKE LEDGE TRAIL
within the Cedar River Municipal Watershed

Level: Easy/Moderate

Total Distance: 3.0 miles

Hiking Time: 1.5 hours

Elevation Gain: 1,200 feet

Summary: A very popular short climb to a scenic viewpoint atop Rattlesnake Ledge.

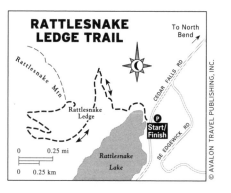

Rattlesnake Ledge Trail is one of the Seattle region's most popular hikes because it's short, easily accessed, and quite nice. The hike is a short climb to an immense outcropping of rock that offers great views of the surrounding area. The trail is new, built by Washington Trails Association and EarthCorps crews in conjunction with Mountains to Sound Greenway Trust and the City of Seattle. The new trail is a vast improvement over the old, which was essentially a straight-up assault on the hill. Now a consistent, manageable, and wide grade whisks hundreds of hikers to the ledge each day.

Rattlesnake Ledge Trail is straightforward and not overly difficult. The hike is a steady climb from start to finish but is easy enough for even novice hikers to tough it out. Expect company on the trail on any day and in any season—summer weekends are particularly busy. In July, Rattlesnake Lake annually hosts Trailfest, a celebration of hiking in the Northwest with kid-oriented education on outdoor safety.

The route to Rattlesnake Ledge starts at Rattlesnake Lake in the Cedar River watershed—from the parking lot, walk around the right side of the lake to the actual trailhead. The trail passes through second-growth forest rich in undergrowth flowers and ferns before making a traverse of the hillside. Occasional views can be had through the trees, but the best views are saved for the end of the hike at Rattlesnake Ledge (1.5 miles). The rocky ledge literally drops straight down, so take care with dogs and children. Views extend across the Snoqualmie Valley to Mount Si and eastward into the watershed, the source of Seattle's drinking water. This is a great place for a picnic and a little sunbathing.

Directions

From Seattle, drive east on I-90 to Exit 32/468th Avenue. Turn right on 468th Avenue (it becomes Southeast Edgewick Road) and drive five miles to the signed trailhead at Rattlesnake Lake.

Information and Contact

This trail is usually accessible year-round and is open to hikers and leashed dogs. Permits are not required. Parking and access are free. For topographic maps, ask Green Trails for No. 205S, Rattlesnake Mountain, or ask the USGS for North Bend. For more information, contact Cedar River Watershed Education Center, 425/831-6780.

2 TWIN FALLS
Olallie State Park

BEST ◖

🏞️ 🐴 👫

Level: Easy

Total Distance: 2.6 miles

Hiking Time: 1.5 hours

Elevation Gain: 200 feet

Summary: A short, easy trail through old-growth forest to a set of great waterfalls.

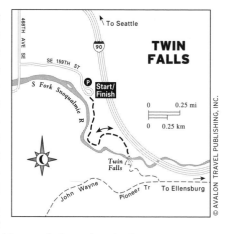

Twin Falls Trail makes an excellent winter hike, when high-country trails are covered with the excessive white of winter's work and the rivers are flowing with Washington's most ordinary commodity: rain. Twin Falls are much more than just a pair; rather, the South Fork of the Snoqualmie River makes a series of cascades that concludes with an impressive plummet of more than 150 feet. The trail is easy going for hikers of all abilities. The journey is nothing to shake your head at, either, as it passes through old-growth forest beside the noisy river.

Well-maintained Twin Falls Trail ambles alongside the South Fork Snoqualmie River to the falls. Several enormous cedars line the trail, left behind because they were too difficult to access. A number of boardwalks and bridges are strategically placed to keep feet dry in even the wettest of weather. Several switchbacks interrupt the easy pace as the trail climbs a minor ridge (0.6 mile). The trail drops to a granddaddy western red cedar (0.8 mile), the largest tree in an already impressive grove. The trail then makes a short, final climb to a pair of viewpoints.

The first, lower viewpoint (1.2 miles) sits on the edge of a cliff, opposite the largest of the falls. Here, a sturdy platform offers a misty view of the falls. Above, a bridge spans the river in the midst of the cascades (1.3 miles). Over centuries the river has cut through the solid granite bedrock, carving out numerous pools where the water swirls tempestuously. The best times to visit are in the winter and spring, when more than 75,000 gallons of water flow over the falls each minute. During dry summers, this torrent dwindles to just 200 gallons per minute.

Options

The trail continues beyond the falls and connects to John Wayne Pioneer Trail (1.7 miles), which provides access to a trailhead at Exit 38 (2.5 miles).

Directions

From Seattle, drive east on I-90 to Exit 34. Turn right off the freeway on 468th Avenue Southeast and drive south 0.5 mile to Southeast 159th Street. Turn left and drive 0.5 mile to the signed trailhead in the parking lot at road's end.

Information and Contact

This trail is accessible year-round and is open to hikers and leashed dogs. There is no wheelchair access. A $5 day-use fee is required to park here

South Fork Snoqualmie River

and is payable at the trailhead, or you can get an annual State Parks Pass for $50; contact Washington State Parks and Recreation, 360/902-8500. For topographic maps, ask Green Trails for No. 206, Bandera, or ask the USGS for Chester Morse Lake. For more information, contact Washington State Parks and Recreation, P.O. Box 42650, Olympia, WA 98504-2669, 360/902-8844.

3 LITTLE SI

Mount Si Natural Resources Conservation Area

🏕 🐕 👪

Level: Easy/Moderate

Total Distance: 4.0 miles

Hiking Time: 2.5 hours

Elevation Gain: 1,200 feet

Summary: A short and easy hike to the summit of Little Si and some great views.

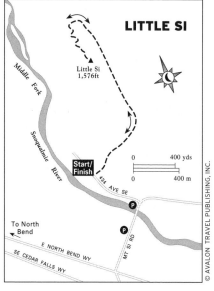

Appropriately named, Little Si is Mount Si in a nutshell. A shorter hike, less of an incline, and fewer people all make this a nice early- or late-season hike when other, more intriguing trails are out of reach because of snow. And like its big sister, Little Si has some great views from its rocky summit. Little Si is a sampler of Cascade hiking, so this is a great hike for kids and folks who are visiting from out of town.

The hike is relatively straightforward. There are a number of unofficial side trails but each junction is signed. Although getting lost on such a short hike would be difficult, it's a good idea to keep track of which direction you came up for the hike down.

Little Si Trail immediately climbs an outcropping of exposed rock and levels out. A small stream is the hike's only source of water (0.6 mile). The trail passes several exposed rock walls (0.8 mile) that are very popular with local rock climbers. Mostly second-growth forest covers the trail, although some granddaddy trees can be seen in places. Soon, the trail begins to curl back around and begin the final climb (1.1 miles).

The summit of Little Si (2.0 miles) is exposed to reveal the surrounding countryside, quickly becoming "North Bend: The Strip Mall." The views from the top extend across the Snoqualmie Valley to Rattlesnake Mountain and up to Mount Si and Mount Washington. Interestingly, the summit has a small community of lodgepole pine trees, a rare occurrence in Western Washington at this elevation. In all, this is a fun and manageable hike for the whole family.

Directions

From Seattle, drive east on I-90 to Exit 32/468th Avenue. Turn left on 468th Avenue and drive to North Bend Way. Turn left and drive to Mount Si Road. Turn right and drive one mile to the trailhead on the left.

Information and Contact

This area is usually accessible March–December. This trail is open to hikers and leashed dogs. Permits are not required. Parking and access are free. For topographic maps, ask Green Trails for No. 206S, Mount Si, or ask the USGS for North Bend. For more information, contact Washington Department of Natural Resources, P.O. Box 47001, Olympia, WA 98504-7001, 360/902-1375.

© CHRIS DUVAL

Just a half hour from Seattle, Little Si is an ideal hike in any season.

4 MOUNT SI

Mount Si Natural Resources Conservation Area

Level: Moderate/Strenuous   **Total Distance:** 8.0 miles

Hiking Time: 5 hours   **Elevation Gain:** 3,200 feet

Summary: Washington's busiest trail climbs steeply throughout its length to a great view of the Cascades out across Snoqualmie Valley.

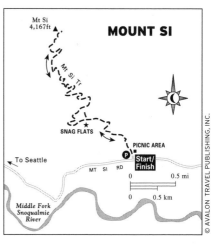

Mount Si is like the Disneyland of Seattle hiking: more crowds than you can shake a stick at. Busloads of folks from the metropolitan area descend upon this mountain, the closest high peak to Seattle. It's literally the most heavily used trail in the state. Experienced and novice hikers alike come here for the views of the Cascades, Seattle, and Puget Sound Basin. The trail is steep and at times rocky, often used by folks as a late-spring training hike for the upcoming summer. It's certainly not an ideal trail for those seeking wilderness exploration, but it scratches the itch for a wooded hike and commanding views.

Mount Si Trail is a continuous climb through the forest. Views into the Snoqualmie River Valley are few until the top. From the trailhead, the trail climbs steadily but not steeply up the hillside. For the first two miles, the tread is in good shape as a result of recent repairs. The trail's only break occurs when it arrives at a junction at Snag Flats (1.8 miles). Taking a right at the junction provides a short side trip (200 feet) to a refreshing stream. The main trail follows the left fork, where it levels out at Snag Flats. A small plateau on the slopes of Mount Si, the forest here was nearly wiped out by a forest fire 100 years ago. Although killed by the fire, a few large snags (dead trees) remain standing and lend the place its name. Extensive puncheon and turnpike installed by EarthCorps crews (including yours truly) help keep feet dry in this muddy section.

From Snag Flats, the trail gets back to business and does nothing but climb. The tread deteriorates from this point on, becoming strewn with rocks and

chilling out at Snag Flats

roots in places. As Washington's busiest trail, summer weekends can feel like rush-hour traffic on the trail, and the toll of such high use is readily apparent. Mount Si Trail eventually breaks out of the forest (3.8 miles) into an open boulder field with salmon berry and beargrass (4.0 miles). The views are spectacular, taking in the Cascades in the east across the Snoqualmie Valley to Seattle and Puget Sound in the west.

This open boulder field is not the summit, but it is the turnaround point for the hike. The true summit of Mount Si is called the Haystack, a large rock outcropping jutting up into the sky. Climbing the Haystack is a difficult and technical rock scramble. It can be dangerous in all seasons, especially when icy. It is best left for those with rock-climbing experience.

Directions

From Seattle, drive east on I-90 to Exit 32/468th Avenue. At the off-ramp, turn left on 468th Avenue and drive to North Bend Way. Turn left and drive to Mount Si Road. Turn right and drive four miles to a discreetly signed gravel road on the left. This is the entrance to the parking lot and trailhead.

Information and Contact

This trail is usually accessible April–November and is open to hikers and leashed dogs. Permits are not required. Parking and access are free. For topographic maps, ask Green Trails for No. 206S, Mount Si, or ask the USGS for Mount Si and Chester Morse Lake. For more information, contact Washington Department of Natural Resources, P.O. Box 47001, Olympia, WA 98504-7001, 360/902-1375.

5 MIDDLE FORK SNOQUALMIE RIVER

Mount Baker-Snoqualmie National Forest

Level: Easy

Hiking Time: 6 hours

Total Distance: 10.8 miles

Elevation Gain: 600 feet

Summary: A family-friendly hike along the dramatic Middle Fork Snoqualmie River with patches of old-growth and views.

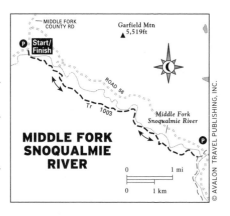

The Middle Fork of the Snoqualmie River is a fantastic trail close to the Seattle area and accessible year-round. Easy to navigate and family-friendly, this hike has a little bit of everything. The trail is enveloped by a lush, mossy forest, although views of the surrounding peaks are frequent. Much of the forest is second-growth, but there are several great stands of old-growth timber. Although much of the route runs along the hillside above the river, the trail dips to the Middle Fork's banks several times. The Middle Fork is great in any season. It rarely gets snow, making it an excellent escape during the winter, and its fall colors are first-rate.

From Middle Fork trailhead, the trail quickly crosses the river on Gateway Bridge, one of the most beautiful backcountry bridges in our region. The trail runs along the river beneath a wall of granite with views up to the massive wall of Mount Garfield. It then enters the forest and moves away from the river, beneath the large wall of Stegosaurus Butte visible through the trees (0.6 mile). Occasionally the trail utilizes an old railroad grade built to haul out the massive timber logged from the valley. The trail is never steep–hikers of all abilities will have no difficulties. In recent years, the Forest Service has invested considerable resources into improving the trail. Numerous wooden structures, like bridges, boardwalks, and turnpikes, are evidence of the hard work put into this beloved trail.

After crossing the small stream from Nine Hour Lake (2.1 miles), the trail finally revisits the riverbanks (3.0 miles). There are several good sites for a rest and picnic in the next quarter mile. If you're not committed to the entire hike, this is an ideal place to turn around. Beyond this point, Middle Fork Trail meanders

© SCOTT LEONARD

A section of Middle Fork Trail runs along a rocky cliff above the river.

through stands of old-growth western hemlock and Douglas fir. This is a wild stretch of trail—elk and bear are not uncommon wildlife encounters. A large bridge crosses Cripple Creek as it cascades over a series of enormous boulders (4.6 miles). The hike ends at the third large bridge of the day. Turn left at the trail's first junction—a sign points left to Dingford Creek and Middle Fork Road. An impressive wooden bridge spans the Middle Fork Snoqualmie River as it roars over a series of large rapids. This is the recommended turnaround point.

Directions

From Seattle, drive east on I-90 to Exit 34. Turn left onto 468th Avenue North and drive 0.5 mile to SE Middle Fork Road. Turn right and drive two miles (via the left fork in the road) to a stop sign at Valley Camp. Turn left on SE Middle Fork Road, which becomes Forest Service Road 56, which is surfaced with gravel but marred by potholes. It is rarely inaccessible. At 12 miles on the right is signed Middle Fork trailhead with a large parking lot.

Information and Contact

This trail is accessible year-round and is open to hikers, leashed dogs, and horses—mountain bikes are not allowed. A federal Northwest Forest Pass is required to park here. For a map of Mount Baker–Snoqualmie National Forest, contact the Outdoor Recreation Information Center at the downtown Seattle REI. For topographic maps, ask Green Trails for No. 174, Mount Si, and No. 175, Skykomish, or ask the USGS for Lake Phillipa and Snoqualmie Lake. For more information, contact Mount Baker–Snoqualmie National Forest, North Bend Ranger Station, 42404 Southeast North Bend Way, North Bend, WA 98045, 425/888-1421.

6 HESTER LAKE
in the Alpine Lakes Wilderness of Mount Baker-Snoqualmie National Forest

Level: Moderate/Strenuous   **Total Distance:** 11.0 miles

Hiking Time: 6 hours   **Elevation Gain:** 2,500 feet

Summary: A rugged, remote, and lightly traveled trail to Hester Lake and some impressive views.

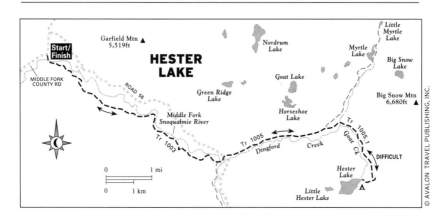

Hester Lake shares three miles of Dingford Creek Trail with the hike to Myrtle Lake, which naturally creates comparisons between the two backcountry lakes. In contrast to the popular Myrtle Lake hike, the trail to Hester Lake is less traveled and feels much wilder. At times the route is difficult to follow, and there is a short scramble near the end. Tucked away in the heart of the Alpine Lakes Wilderness, this challenging hike pays off at the end with large Hester Lake in a forested basin. The trail is best suited to hikers prepared for and seeking a true backcountry experience.

The first half of the hike is straightforward. From the trailhead, Dingford Creek Trail makes a steep ascent through second-growth forest. The roar of Dingford Creek over falls is heard but is out of sight from the trail. The route soon enters the Alpine Lakes Wilderness (1.0 mile) and crosses a stream at a small waterfall (1.3 miles) before easing up. Old-growth Douglas fir, western hemlock, and Pacific silver fir line the route, the hike's best section of trail. The grade is a gentle but steady ascent. The trail passes Goat Creek (2.0 miles) before reaching a signed junction for Hester Lake (3.0 miles).

Turn right on Hester Lake Trail and soon make a ford of Dingford Creek (3.3 miles). The ford is usually quite manageable. Beyond here, though, the trail gets rough. Overgrown brush and muddy spots are the norm in every season. The trail passes through several swampy segments as it climbs up the valley. At one point the trail fades out (about 4.3 miles), but a sign nailed to a tree points the way. The trail crosses the creek several times at manageable fords. Just as the challenge seems overwhelming, the trail finds the outlet of Hester Lake. Mount Price looms over the forested basin. Anglers love the lake for its stocked rainbow trout, but other visitors are sure to be few and far between. There are several campsites scattered around the lake, making this an excellent overnight trip.

Directions

From Seattle, drive east on I-90 to Exit 34. Turn left onto 468th Avenue North and drive 0.5 mile to SE Middle Fork Road. Turn right and drive two miles (via the left fork in the road) to a stop sign at Valley Camp. Turn left on SE Middle Fork Road, which becomes Forest Service Road 56. The first 12 miles are surfaced with gravel but marred by potholes. The last seven miles are pretty rough and subject to washouts. A passenger car can usually make the drive. At 12 miles, pass Middle Fork trailhead. At 12.5 miles, cross the Taylor River and take the hard right immediately following (this is still the Middle Fork Road). At 19 miles is Dingford Creek trailhead at a very wide turnout on the right. The trail is discreetly signed on the uphill side of the road.

Information and Contact

This trail is accessible July–early November and is open to hikers and leashed dogs. A federal Northwest Forest Pass is required to park here. For a map of Mount Baker–Snoqualmie National Forest, contact the Outdoor Recreation Information Center at the downtown Seattle REI. For topographic maps, ask Green Trails for No. 175, Skykomish, or ask the USGS for Snoqualmie Lake and Big Snow Mountain. For more information, contact Mount Baker–Snoqualmie National Forest, North Bend Ranger Station, 42404 Southeast North Bend Way, North Bend, WA 98045, 425/888-1421.

7 MYRTLE LAKE

in the Alpine Lake Wilderness of Mount Baker-Snoqualmie National Forest

Level: Moderate   **Total Distance:** 11.0 miles

Hiking Time: 6 hours   **Elevation Gain:** 2,400 feet

Summary: A quiet hike through great old-growth forest to forested but scenic Myrtle Lake in the heart of the Alpine Lakes Wilderness.

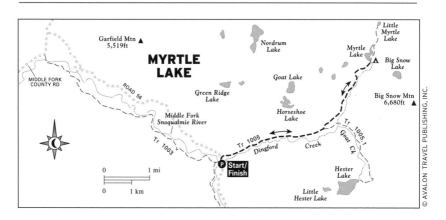

Dingford Creek Trail is the starting point for a pair of hikes to backcountry lakes. The trail splits at 3.0 miles with routes to Hester and Myrtle Lakes. In contrast to the wild hike to Hester, the trip to Myrtle Lake is rather straightforward. Myrtle Lake follows an easier, more defined trail. Subsequently, Myrtle Lake sees considerably more use than Hester Lake. Traveling through old-growth forest along the rumbling Dingford Creek, the trail finds Myrtle Lake in a forested basin with views of surrounding peaks and mountains. Whether the plan is to fish, scramble to other surrounding lakes, or just enjoy the views at Myrtle Lake, this is a well-regarded hike.

From the trailhead, Dingford Creek Trail makes a steep ascent through second-growth forest where Dingford Creek is noisy but mostly out of sight. Thankfully this is the steepest section of the hike. The trail enters the Alpine Lakes Wilderness (1.0 mile) and crosses a small stream (1.3 miles) before easing up. The forest is old-growth hemlock and Pacific silver fir—it's a peaceful walk through a beautiful forest. The grade is a gentle but steady ascent. The trail passes Goat Creek (2.0 miles) before reaching a signed junction for Hester Lake (3.0 miles).

Stay to the left on Dingford Creek Trail as it continues the climb up the valley. This section of trail is notoriously muddy in places—the number of boots far exceeds the maintenance given the trail. The trail makes another easy creek crossing (4.2 miles) and runs beside the roar of Dingford Creek. Dingford Creek Trail reaches the shores of Myrtle Lake (5.5 miles) as the forest gradually opens to the perfect setting for Myrtle Lake. Amply stocked with trout, the lake is popular with anglers. Big Snow Mountain towers over Myrtle's waters from the southeast. There are several campsites located around the lake—this is an easy overnight backpacking trip. Myrtle Lake is also a great snowshoe trip in the winter.

Options
Folks with off-trail experience can access any of the numerous lakes located near Myrtle Lake. Dingford Creek Trail continues around Myrtle Lake and climbs beside the creek to Little Myrtle Lake (6.7 miles). Other small footpaths lead from Myrtle Lake to impressive Big Snow and Snowflake Lakes to the east (6.8 miles). From Myrtle Lake, a faint trail heads west to the trio of Merlin, Nimue, and Le Fay Lakes (6.0 miles).

Directions
From Seattle, drive east on I-90 to Exit 34. Turn left onto 468th Avenue North and drive 0.5 mile to SE Middle Fork Road. Turn right and drive two miles (via the left fork in the road) to a stop sign at Valley Camp. Turn left on SE Middle Fork Road, which becomes Forest Service Road 56. The first 12 miles are surfaced with gravel but marred by potholes. The last seven miles are pretty rough and subject to washouts. A passenger car can usually make the drive. At 12 miles, pass Middle Fork trailhead. At 12.5 miles, cross the Taylor River and take the hard right immediately following (this is still the Middle Fork Road). At 19 miles is Dingford Creek trailhead at a very wide turnout on the right. The trail is discreetly signed on the uphill side of the road.

Information and Contact
This trail is accessible July–early November and is open to hikers and leashed dogs. A federal Northwest Forest Pass is required to park here. For a map of Mount Baker–Snoqualmie National Forest, contact the Outdoor Recreation Information Center at the downtown Seattle REI. For topographic maps, ask Green Trails for No. 175, Skykomish, or ask the USGS for Snoqualmie Lake and Big Snow Mountain. For more information, contact Mount Baker–Snoqualmie National Forest, North Bend Ranger Station, 42404 Southeast North Bend Way, North Bend, WA 98045, 425/888-1421.

8 BANDERA MOUNTAIN
in the Alpine Lakes Wilderness of Mount Baker-Snoqualmie
National Forest

🏠 🏕 🐾 🎿

Level: Moderate/Strenuous

Hiking Time: 5 hours

Total Distance: 7.0 miles

Elevation Gain: 3,100 feet

Summary: A challenging climb through forest and meadows to the summit of Bandera Mountain and far-flung views of the Cascades.

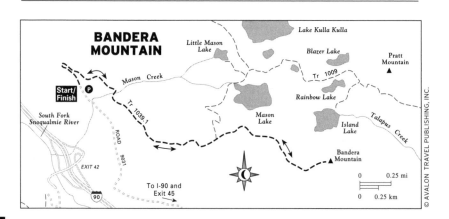

Bandera has a reputation for two things: a steep, difficult ascent and breath-taking panoramic views. Both are accurate descriptions of this popular hike. The only thing easy about a trip to Bandera Mountain is the access to its trailhead—just 40 minutes from Seattle. In spite of the hard work, the hike to Bandera Mountain is worth every step. The trail spends the majority of time in open meadows, with constant views. And standing atop the summit of Bandera is, not surprisingly, a satisfying experience.

The route to Bandera Mountain follows Ira Spring Trail for the first half of the hike. This section of trail begins as an old logging road which traverses the hillside in the forest. The trail crosses several small streams, which are better appreciated on the return trip. The Forest Service recently completed several seasons of work on this trail, much improving the route and the tread. The effort of countless volunteers appears in the form of narrow, real trail (1.2 miles) which leaves the roadbed behind but continues to traverse the lower slopes of Bandera Mountain.

Ira Spring Trail breaks out of the forest and onto the exposed hillside (2.0 miles). From here on, the hike travels through open terrain. Hot summer days make the taxing climb all the more difficult. It's important to pack extra water and sunscreen if the sun is out—unprepared hikers pay the price. In return for the extra sun, Mount Rainier appears to the south and never leaves the party.

Ira Spring Trail reaches a signed junction with Bandera Mountain Trail (2.2 miles). Turn right as the trail immediately gets nasty and climbs sharply through meadows of mountain ash and bear grass. The ascent is steep and sometimes hand over hand. A false summit (3.0 miles) is a disappointment, but the true summit has never been closer. The trail reaches the summit (3.5 miles), nearly a mile in the sky (5,240 feet). The views of the Cascades extend for miles in every direction.

the junction for Mason Lake and Bandera Mountain

Options

Hikers who are in good shape and looking for extra miles can combine a hike to Bandera Mountain with a trip to Mason Lake and other nearby lakes. This add-on option is detailed in the Mason Lake listing (see next listing)—Ira Spring Trail continues from the junction with Bandera Mountain Trail and climbs gently to Mason, Rainbow, and finally Island Lakes. This summit/lake combo is a total of 9.0 miles.

Directions

From Seattle, drive east on I-90 to Exit 45/Forest Service Road 9030. Turn left (north, over the freeway) to Forest Service Road 9030. Turn left and drive left 0.5 mile to Forest Service Road 9031. Veer left on Forest Service Road 9031 and drive four miles to the trailhead at road's end.

Information and Contact

This trail is accessible May–October and is open to hikers and leashed dogs. A federal Northwest Forest Pass is required to park here. A free wilderness permit is also required to hike here and is available at the trailhead. For a map of Mount Baker–Snoqualmie National Forest, contact the Outdoor Recreation Information Center at the downtown Seattle REI. For topographic maps, ask Green Trails for No. 206, Bandera, or ask the USGS for Bandera. For more information, contact Mount Baker–Snoqualmie National Forest, North Bend Ranger Station, 42404 Southeast North Bend Way, North Bend, WA 98045, 425/888-1421.

9 MASON LAKE

in the Alpine Lakes Wilderness of Mount Baker-Snoqualmie
National Forest

Level: Moderate

Hiking Time: 4 hours

Total Distance: 6.6 miles

Elevation Gain: 2,500 feet

Summary: A new trail passes through expansive hillside meadows to a large wooded basin holding eight picturesque lakes.

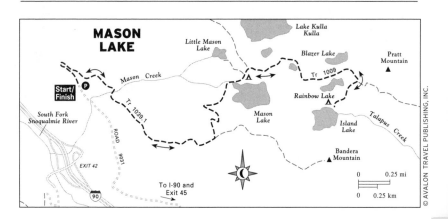

This popular hike is a great example of where Alpine Lakes Wilderness gets its name. Recently reconstructed Ira Spring Trail leads to a high basin holding eight beautiful lakes. The new trail commemorates one of Washington's strongest wilderness advocates, the late trail guru Ira Spring. The well-known photographer campaigned over many years for better access to Mason Lake, and his efforts finally paid off several years after he passed away. The new trail is well-constructed and has greatly improved the trip to Mason Lake. It is fitting that such a beautiful trail be named for a man like Ira Spring.

Ira Spring Trail begins as it always has, on an old logging road. The trail passes a couple small streams before encountering the hard work of the numerous volunteers. This is where the route leaves the road and turns into good single-track trail (1.2 miles). The new section continues climbing steadily as it breaks out of the forest and onto the open hillside. Mount Rainier is a gorgeous sight to the south.

Ira Spring Trail reaches a junction with Bandera Mountain Trail (2.3 miles); stay to the left on Ira Spring Trail as it climbs gently through open meadows and boulder fields. This section of trail catches fire with wildflowers in

The recently reconstructed trail to Mason Lake and Bandera Mountain offers plenty of scenic views.

early summer. A trip in August may yield tasty huckleberries. And those loud whistles aren't lost construction workers, just marmots giving a warning call to their buddies.

The trail reaches the wilderness boundary as it crests a small ridgeline (2.5 miles) and then descends 500 feet to a wide, forested basin and Mason Lake (3.2 miles). Fields of heather and huckleberries are prolific, as are the blackflies and mosquitoes in early summer. Mason Lake is a fine place to turn around, but a walk through the basin to the other lakes is a well-spent afternoon. The lakes are prime swimming holes, deep, cool, and sunny. The basin sees lots of use, so please stay on trail or hard surfaces near the lakes.

Beyond Mason Lake, Ira Spring Trail encounters Little Mason Lake Trail (3.3 miles), a short trip to a small lake. Ira Spring Trail ends at a junction with Mount Defiance Trail (3.4 miles). Take a right as Mount Defiance Trail wanders through the wooded basin. Side trails lead to Lake Kulla Kulla (3.7 miles), Rainbow Lake (4.4 miles), Blazer Lake (4.6 miles), and Island Lake (4.7 miles). The lakes are stocked with trout, and each has campsites for overnight visits.

Options

Hikers with an itch to bag a summit and to take in some (more) views will love a side trip to Mount Defiance. At 5,584 feet, this is one of the tallest peaks in the area. From the junction at Mason Lake, turn left on Mount Defiance Trail and climb 1.7 miles to just below the peak, where a small social trail leads to the summit.

Directions

From Seattle, drive east on I-90 to Exit 45/Forest Service Road 9030. Turn left (north, over the freeway) to Forest Service Road 9030. Turn left and drive left 0.5 mile to Forest Service Road 9031. Veer left on Forest Service Road 9031 and drive four miles to the trailhead at road's end.

Information and Contact

This trail is accessible May–October and is open to hikers and leashed dogs. A federal Northwest Forest Pass is required to park here. A free wilderness permit is also required to hike here and is available at the trailhead. For a map of Mount Baker–Snoqualmie National Forest, contact the Outdoor Recreation Information Center at the downtown Seattle REI. For topographic maps, ask Green Trails for No. 206, Bandera, or ask the USGS for Bandera. For more information, contact Mount Baker–Snoqualmie National Forest, North Bend Ranger Station, 42404 Southeast North Bend Way, North Bend, WA 98045, 425/888-1421.

10 TALAPUS LAKE BEST 【

in the Alpine Lakes Wilderness of Mount Baker-Snoqualmie National Forest

Level: Easy/Moderate

Hiking Time: 2.5 hours

Total Distance: 4.4 miles

Elevation Gain: 800 feet

Summary: An excellent hike for families up to rocky Talapus Lake with an option for slightly more challenging Olallie Lake.

Talapus Lake is the ideal hike for families with small children. An elevation gain of just 800 feet is spread over 2.2 miles, a grade gentle enough for the youngest of hikers. Young or old, Talapus Lake is a great introduction to the Alpine Lakes Wilderness. The trail lazily switchbacks through shady forest to the shores of Talapus Lake. Less than an hour's drive from Seattle, the hike is accessible but busy—the trail is one of the most popular hikes in the Alpine Lakes Wilderness, and crowds can be as thick as the mosquitoes on summer weekends.

Talapus Lake Trail begins by following an old roadbed but soon transitions to single-track trail (0.3 mile). At first the forest is dense and dark, but it gradually opens. The shade is a welcome respite from the hot sun. In spite of the heavy traffic, the trail is in good shape. The tread is well-maintained, and wooden structures span streams and marshy areas.

Talapus Lake Trail eventually encounters Talapus Creek (1.7 miles), a roaring torrent in spring and early summer, just before entering Alpine Lakes Wilderness. The trail then crosses the creek (1.9 miles) and arrives at the shores of Talapus Lake (2.2 miles). The lake rests within a large, rocky basin ringed by forest. The area has seen lots of overuse—be sure to stick to maintained trails and out of restoration plots. There are many good camping spots around the lake, but they go very quickly during the summer.

© AVALON TRAVEL PUBLISHING, INC.

Options

Olallie Lake is an easy and scenic option for a slightly longer hike. Less than a mile from Talapus, the lake has considerably thinner crowds. From Talapus Lake, continue on the main Talapus Lake Trail as it skirts the east side of the lake and continues climbing up the hillside. The trail reaches a junction with Pratt Lake Trail at a stream crossing (2.5 miles from the trailhead). Stay to the left (don't cross the stream) and continue climbing gently through old forest to the forested shores of Olallie Lake. Several campsites ring the lake.

Talapus Lake Trail is an ideal hike for families.

Directions

From Seattle, drive east on I-90 to Exit 45/USFS Road 9030. From the off-ramp, turn left (north) and drive 0.9 mile to a fork in the road. Turn right onto Forest Service Road 9030 and drive 3.5 miles to the parking lot and signed trailhead at the road's end. On summer weekends, the parking lot fills quickly—you may have to park down the road and walk to the trailhead.

Information and Contact

This trail is accessible May–October and is open to hikers and leashed dogs. A federal Northwest Forest Pass is required to park here. A free wilderness permit is also required to hike here and is available at the trailhead. For a map of Mount Baker–Snoqualmie National Forest, contact the Outdoor Recreation Information Center at the downtown Seattle REI. For topographic maps, ask Green Trails for No. 206, Bandera, or ask the USGS for Bandera. For more information, contact Mount Baker–Snoqualmie National Forest, North Bend Ranger Station, 42404 Southeast North Bend Way, North Bend, WA 98045, 425/888-1421.

11 GRANITE MOUNTAIN   BEST ☾

in the Alpine Lakes Wilderness of Mount Baker-Snoqualmie National Forest

🎒 🌸 ⚙ 🐴 🎿

Level: Strenuous   **Total Distance:** 8.6 miles

Hiking Time: 6 hours   **Elevation Gain:** 3,900 feet

Summary: This is the toughest hike in the I-90 corridor and offers insane views from a lookout atop Granite Summit.

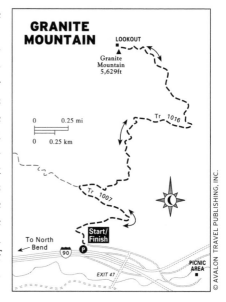

Let's not mince words: Granite Mountain Trail is a hell of a climb. In fact, this is about the most difficult trail in the book. The trail ascends nearly 4,000 feet in just over four miles. That is what is known as a good workout. Fortunately, Granite Mountain Trail spends miles in broad meadows with abundant views of surrounding peaks. All of the hard work is worth it, as Granite Mountain is one of the best summit views in the region. The summit is home to the last functioning fire lookout operated by the Forest Service in the area. If the Forest Service spends time here, you know it has views.

Before you leave home, be prepared for a hot, difficult hike. Be armed with extra water—there's none to be found along the way. Sunscreen is a must on sunny days. Much of Granite Mountain Trail travels through exposed terrain with no forest to provide shade, making the hike twice as difficult when the sun beats down on this southern slope. Know that the elevation gain is serious business—beginning hikers just won't find this hike fun.

The route to Granite Mountain begins on Pratt Lake Trail. Follow this trail from the trailhead as it gently climbs through shady forest. Enjoy the cover while it lasts. Granite Mountain Trail begins at the first junction (1.2 miles), leading off to the right. The aggressive ascent soon turns downright nasty as the trail begins a relentless climb up the hillside. Switchback after switchback

The upper half of Granite Mountain Trail mostly traverses meadows and offers breath-taking views.

quickly rises above the valley, with I-90 far below. Thank goodness for the grand view of Mount Rainier.

The trail offers a quick breather as it levels out briefly (2.6 miles) but soon gets back to business. Another segment of switchbacks leads into a beautiful basin along the eastern side of Granite Mountain. This is the best section of the hike. Enormous granite boulders lie scattered throughout the meadows. Those scurrying little balls of fur are marmots. If you catch one by surprise, it's sure to give its signature whistle.

After a final steep section, the trail finally arrives at the summit. All of the Snoqualmie-area peaks are on parade, as are Mount Baker and Glacier Peak, on clear days. Crystal and Denny Lakes beg you to come jump in their waters, but unfortunately they're inaccessible. Early summer is the ideal time to visit. Wildflowers are in bloom and the last vestiges of winter's snow add definition to the surrounding mountains.

Directions

From Seattle, drive east on I-90 to Exit 47, signed Denny Creek/Asahel Curtis. Turn left (north) from the off-ramp and turn left at the T in the road. Drive 0.5 mile to the signed trailhead at the end of the road.

Information and Contact

This trail is accessible May–October and is open to hikers and leashed dogs. A federal Northwest Forest Pass is required to park here. For a map of Mount Baker–Snoqualmie National Forest, contact the Outdoor Recreation Information Center at the downtown Seattle REI. For topographic maps, ask Green Trails for No. 207, Snoqualmie Pass, or ask the USGS for Snoqualmie Pass. For more information, contact Mount Baker–Snoqualmie National Forest, North Bend Ranger Station, 42404 Southeast North Bend Way, North Bend, WA 98045, 425/888-1421.

12 PRATT LAKE   BEST (C

in the Alpine Lakes Wilderness of Mount Baker-Snoqualmie
National Forest

🦌 🛶 🏕 ⛷

Level: Moderate   **Total Distance:** 11.4 miles

Hiking Time: 7 hours   **Elevation Gain:** 3,200 feet

Summary: A relatively unknown hike in the I-90 corridor, Pratt Lake Trail climbs then drops through great forest to this large lake.

Pratt Lake is one of the nicest but least-visited destinations in Alpine Lakes Wilderness. The journey to the lake is just as great as the destination. Great forests, views of Mount Rainier, berries for everyone, and lots of lakeshore to explore are yours for the enjoying. What's more is that there are often few people along this route. That's amazing, since it is easily one of the best loops anywhere near I-90 and Seattle.

Pratt Lake Trail begins in the shade of forest, a welcome friend on hot summer days. The well-maintained path climbs gently, crossing several small creeks on the flank of Granite Mountain. There are three junctions along the way to Pratt Lake. Stay to the left at the first signed junction with Granite Mountain Trail (1.2 miles). The trail enters the wilderness (2.6 miles), where the best is yet to come. The second junction (3.1 miles) is the turnoff for Olallie and Talapus Lakes—stay to the right on Pratt Lake Trail.

Pratt Lake Trail now contours above Olallie Lake, and the forest breaks for an amazing view of Mount Rainier. This is where the trail crests the ridge and reaches the final junction (4.3 miles). To the left along the ridge is Mount Defiance Trail, which leads to Mason Lakes and, of course, Mount Defiance. Head to the right as Pratt Lake Trail drops through stands of big trees and fields of granite boulders. The chirping you hear is picas, little creatures who live in the rocks, saying hello. Mount Roosevelt stands out across from the basin, above Pratt Lake.

The trail winds around the east side of Pratt Lake and finally reaches the lakeshore near its outlet at the north end of the lake (5.7 miles). Remnants of abandoned Pratt River Trail are on the western shore, ripe for exploration for those with a sense of adventure. In addition to being a good day hike, Pratt Lake is a great beginner's backpacking trip—there are numerous campsites here. Campfires are not allowed in either lake basin—be sure to bring backcountry stoves. At night, with the moon and stars at play in the sky, this place seems very far away from everything, yet it is less than an hour from Seattle.

Options
A trip combining Pratt Lake and Denny Creek Trails is an excellent but long day hike (13.7 miles) or a great backpacking trip. Unfortunately, the separate trailheads add another four miles of road hiking—a car drop makes this much easier. From Pratt Lake (5.7 miles), hike east on Melakwa Lake Trail past my favorite Alpine Lakes swimming hole at Lower Tuscohatchie Lake (6.2 miles), up to Melakwa Lake (9.2 miles), and down Denny Creek Trail to the trailhead (13.7 miles). Be sure to bring a map for this hike.

Directions
From Seattle, drive east on I-90 to Exit 47, signed Denny Creek/Asahel Curtis. Turn left (north) from the off-ramp, pass over the freeway, and turn left at the T in the road. Drive 0.5 mile to the parking lot and signed trailhead.

Information and Contact
This trail is accessible June–October and is open to hikers and leashed dogs. A federal Northwest Forest Pass is required to park here. A free wilderness permit is also required to hike here and is available at the trailhead. For a map of Mount Baker–Snoqualmie National Forest, contact the Outdoor Recreation Information Center at the downtown Seattle REI. For topographic maps, ask Green Trails for No. 206, Bandera, and No. 207, Snoqualmie Pass, or ask the USGS for Bandera. For more information, contact Mount Baker–Snoqualmie National Forest, North Bend Ranger Station, 42404 Southeast North Bend Way, North Bend, WA 98045, 425/888-1421.

13 ANNETTE LAKE   BEST [
Mount Baker-Snoqualmie National Forest

🛶 ⛷ 🐎 👫 🚵

Level: Moderate   **Total Distance:** 7.0 miles

Hiking Time: 4 hours   **Elevation Gain:** 1,900 feet

Summary: Easily accessed from I-90, this is a moderate hike through shady old-growth forest to beautiful, wooded Annette Lake.

Step by step, the trail to Annette Lake adds up to a really nice hike. Climbing through a striking forest of old trees, the trail finds Annette Lake surrounded in her basin by rocky peaks and fed by a waterfall. For such great scenery, the hike is fairly accessible. The trail is a moderate but persistent ascent to Annette Lake—it's not a cakewalk but it's not excessively strenuous either. Naturally, this hike is very popular—less than an hour from Seattle and just off of the interstate, the trail attracts more than its fair share of visitors. Summer weekends are always busy.

Annette Lake Trail barely leaves the trailhead before it gets interesting. Roaring Humpback Creek cascades over large boulders where the trail crosses it on a large, newly built wooden bridge (0.2 mile). The trail gently climbs, first crossing a decommissioned logging road (0.3 mile) and then encountering the Iron Horse Trail (0.7 mile), a rails-to-trails project running from Cle Elum to Seattle.

After crossing the Iron Horse, the trail focuses on putting elevation behind it. A series of switchbacks (1.5 miles) is the toughest section, but the grade is not difficult. By this point, the hike has become much better—the forest is unscathed by logging and opens up considerably. Large hemlocks and firs filter out the sunlight, a welcome favor on really hot days. Compared to other hikes with long exposed sections, Annette Lake Trail is a cool breeze.

Throughout the hike, the tread is well-maintained and wide enough to accommodate the summer traffic. Stream crossings and a marsh are negotiated by solid wooden structures. There is plenty of water along the trail to keep four-legged companions well-hydrated. You know you're nearing Annette Lake when several small avalanche chutes interrupt the forest (3.1 miles). The views across to the granite walls of Humpback Mountain are especially great. At this point, the trail levels out and even drops slightly to Annette Lake (3.5 miles). The lake sits between Silver Peak and Abiel Peak, with steep cliffs dropping into the old forest that surrounds the lake. It's not your typically deep blue subalpine lake, but it's an inviting swimming hole nonetheless on hot days. Plus, it makes for some decent fishing.

The hike to Annette Lake travels through outstanding old-growth forest.

Directions
From Seattle, drive east on I-90 to Exit 47, signed Denny Creek/Ashael Curtis. Turn right (south) and drive 0.2 mile to the T intersection. Turn left on Forest Service Road 55 and drive 0.5 mile to the signed trailhead at road's end.

Information and Contact
This trail is accessible June–mid-November and is open to hikers and leashed dogs. A federal Northwest Forest Pass is required to park here. A free wilderness permit is also required to hike here and is available at the trailhead. For a map of Mount Baker–Snoqualmie National Forest, contact the Outdoor Recreation Information Center at the downtown Seattle REI. For topographic maps, ask Green Trails for No. 207, Snoqualmie Pass, or ask the USGS for Snoqualmie Pass and Lost Lake. For more information, contact Mount Baker–Snoqualmie National Forest, North Bend Ranger Station, 42404 Southeast North Bend Way, North Bend, WA 98045, 425/888-1421.

14 DENNY CREEK TRAIL TO MELAKWA LAKE

BEST ◖

in the Alpine Lakes Wilderness of Mount Baker-Snoqualmie National Forest

Level: Moderate

Total Distance: 9.0 miles

Hiking Time: 5 hours

Elevation Gain: 2,200 feet

Summary: The best hike within an hour of Seattle, Denny Creek Trail hits up big trees and big waterfalls on the way to picturesque Melakwa Lake.

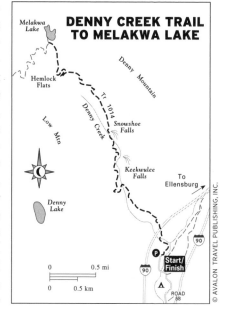

I won't be shy in professing my affection for Denny Creek Trail—this is the most beautiful hike in the I-90 corridor and has many great moments. The hike begins in a forest of big trees and cool shade. As the route climbs through berry patches, two series of incredible waterfalls parallel the trail. And after crossing Hemlock Pass, Melakwa Lake sits within a beautiful, large basin, rimmed by jagged peaks giving way to forests of subalpine trees. This is a perfect introduction to all that the Alpine Lakes Wilderness has to offer. It's also the type of place that will have you revisiting year after year. Be forewarned that this is an extremely popular trail—solitude is rare.

Denny Creek Trail begins along Denny Creek in cool, quiet shade. The trail actually passes beneath the elevated interstate as cars and trucks zoom overhead. The highway overpass preserves important green-space corridors, allowing wildlife to move uninhibited through the forests and providing hikers a much nicer experience.

The trail enters the Alpine Lakes Wilderness and climbs gently until it reaches a large, sturdy wooden bridge spanning Denny Creek (1.0 mile). The creek here runs over large slabs of exposed bedrock and is a favorite splashing hole. This is a good place to turn around if hiking with young children because the trail gains most of its elevation beyond this point.

Denny Creek Trail turns serious after the crossing and begins climbing steadily. The trail gets in a great view of Keekwulee Falls (1.9 miles), which can really roar with snowmelt in late spring. A segment of sharp switchbacks rewards with a view of another beautiful set of falls at Snowshoe Falls (2.5 miles). The forest breaks as the trail switchbacks up through avalanche chutes. Heavy snowpack slides down the hillside each year and prevents trees from taking hold, leaving tasty huckleberry and salmonberry bushes to flourish.

Denny Creek Trail finally reaches Hemlock Pass (4.2 miles) amidst giant mountain hemlocks. Follow the trail as it descends slightly to a junction immediately below Melakwa Lake. Turn right and enter the lake basin, which is pure heaven. This is an ideal swimming hole, with plenty of rock slabs for basking in the sun. Sharp-toothed Chair Peak is the tallest peak of the jagged rim around the basin. Beware of mosquitoes and other biting pests in early summer. There are many campsites at the lake, on both the eastern and western shores. Be sure to stay on footpaths, as the meadows here have taken a beating.

© PATTI BLEIFUSS

Less than an hour from Seattle, Melakwa Lake is a popular final destination.

Directions
From Seattle, drive east on I-90 to Exit 47, signed Denny Creek/Asahel Curtis. Turn left (north) from the off-ramp and turn right at the T in the road. Drive 0.4 mile to Forest Service Road 58. Turn left and drive four miles to the signed trailhead.

Information and Contact
This trail is accessible mid-June–October and is open to hikers and leashed dogs. A federal Northwest Forest Pass is required to park here. A free wilderness permit is also required to hike here and is available at the trailhead. For

a map of Mount Baker–Snoqualmie National Forest, contact the Outdoor Recreation Information Center at the downtown Seattle REI. For topographic maps, ask Green Trails for No. 207, Snoqualmie Pass, or ask the USGS for Snoqualmie Pass. For more information, contact Mount Baker–Snoqualmie National Forest, North Bend Ranger Station, 42404 Southeast North Bend Way, North Bend, WA 98045, 425/888-1421.

15 SNOW LAKE BEST ☾

in the Alpine Lakes Wilderness of Mount Baker-Snoqualmie
National Forest

Level: Easy/Moderate

Hiking Time: 3 hours

Total Distance: 5.6 miles

Elevation Gain: 1,700 feet

Summary: The crowded trail makes an easy trip to subalpine meadows and
large Snow Lake beneath rocky peaks.

Everything about Snow Lake seems larger than life. The lake is one of the largest lakes in the Alpine Lakes Wilderness, a respectable honor. The big basin absorbs the large crowds that make the trek. Big meadows and bigger peaks add to the scenery. It's all large and all exceptionally grand. Part of the lake's high popularity is due to its easy accessibility. The trail is not difficult and works well for families with kids. The hike is nice even if cut short and offers great options for a longer adventure.

Snow Lake Trail gently works its way up the valley to a junction with Source Lake Trail (1.5 miles). This section of trail has an easy grade but repeatedly crosses open rock slides—hiking boots work better than sneakers. These open slides provide great views of the jagged ridge of Denny Mountain, The Tooth, Bryant Peak, and Chair Peak. Already this is a great hike.

At the junction, turn right and begin the hike's main ascent, a series of sharp switchbacks up the exposed hillside, climbing 700 feet in 0.6 mile. The trail crosses the wilderness boundary (2.2 miles) and levels out at the pass (2.3 miles), home to some large mountain hemlocks. This saddle offers good views of Snow Lake below and poses a dilemma. To reach Snow Lake requires giving up 400 feet, so this is the turnaround spot for those who don't feel like hiking down to the lake.

© AVALON TRAVEL PUBLISHING, INC.

From the saddle, Snow Lake Trail drops to the shores of Snow Lake (2.8 miles). It's easy to understand why the lake is so popular—fields of granite, large meadows, and rugged peaks surround the lake. Chair Peak is the most prominent pike of the ragged ridges. There are numerous spots around the lake for a picnic. The lake is one big swimming hole in the summer, but its chilly waters reflect its name. The lake is popular with anglers, too.

Options

Snow Lake isn't the only lake in this basin. For a longer trip, High Lakes Trail accesses a pair of backcountry lakes and is a great addition to this hike. The weekend crowds thin out considerably past Snow Lake. At three miles on Snow Lake Trail, near the northeast corner of Snow Lake, turn left on signed High Lakes Trail. The maintained trail crosses Rock Creek and climbs 800 feet to Gem Lake (5.0 miles) before dropping 1,000 feet to Lower Wildcat Lake (6.9 miles).

Directions

From Seattle, drive east on I-90 to Exit 52/West Summit. Turn left (under the freeway) and left again on Alpental Road. Drive 0.2 mile and turn right on Forest Service Road 9040. Drive 1.5 miles to a large gravel parking lot on the left. The trailhead is on the right.

© CHRIS DUVAL

Snow Lake Trail is one of the most popular hikes in the Mount Baker-Snoqualmie National Forest.

Information and Contact

This trail is accessible July–October and is open to hikers and leashed dogs. A federal Northwest Forest Pass is required to park here. A free wilderness permit is also required to hike here and is available at the trailhead. For a map of Mount Baker–Snoqualmie National Forest, contact the Outdoor Recreation Information Center at the downtown Seattle REI. For topographic maps, ask Green Trails for No. 207, Snoqualmie Pass, or ask the USGS for Snoqualmie Pass. For more information, contact Mount Baker–Snoqualmie National Forest, North Bend Ranger Station, 42404 Southeast North Bend Way, North Bend, WA 98045, 425/888-1421.

1 6 COMMONWEALTH BASIN   BEST ◖

in the Alpine Lakes Wilderness of Mount Baker-Snoqualmie National Forest

🏕 🌸 🐴

Level: Moderate/Strenuous

Hiking Time: 6 hours

Total Distance: 9.0 miles

Elevation Gain: 1,900 feet

Summary: An enjoyable but strenuous hike to scenic meadows and Red Pond in Commonwealth Basin.

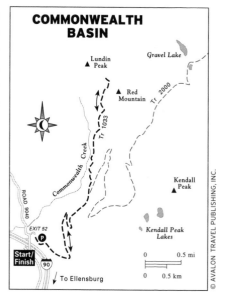

COMMONWEALTH BASIN

© AVALON TRAVEL PUBLISHING, INC.

This is one of the more difficult trails out of the Snoqualmie Pass area. The route climbs gently through outstanding old-growth forest before making a steep, leg-busting climb to the meadows of Commonwealth Basin. Such difficult work is rewarded with views, fields of huckleberries, and an idyllic lunch spot. The trail can be made easier or more difficult. Families will enjoy hiking up the valley through old forests but avoiding the steep ascent. Hikers itching for more will be glad to know that Commonwealth Basin features the option to hike an additional half mile to Red Pass for views to the north.

The first half of the route follows Pacific Crest Trail north from Snoqualmie Pass. Along this stretch, the trail gently and gradually climbs through shady forest of big hemlock and fir. The trail drops slightly before reaching the signed Commonwealth Basin Trail junction (2.5 miles). To this point, the trail sees a lot of traffic, most of which is headed to Kendall Katwalk on the PCT. Commonwealth Basin Trail will feel relatively deserted.

Stick to the left on Commonwealth Basin Trail as the forest gradually opens up and crosses a branch of Commonwealth Creek (3.7 miles). This is a good turnaround for hikers without aspirations for a serious climb—the trail to this point is a good hike in and of itself. From the stream crossing, the trail gets mean and sharply ascends up the hillside through patches of forest. The elevation gain is 800 feet in 0.6 mile. The trail graciously levels out at Commonwealth Basin (4.5

miles) at the bases of Lundin Peak and Red Mountain, which is surprising in how red it is. The views are good and the wildflowers are amazing in early summer. Red Pond is a good lunch spot if not buggy.

Options

If your legs are up to it and you're hungry for a different vista, the climb to Red Pass is recommended. From Red Pond, Commonwealth Basin Trail picks up where it left off—quickly scaling the hillside. The trail ends at Red Pass (5.0 miles), a saddle full of flower meadows between Lundin Peak and Red Mountain. The views to the north include a wide perspective of the Middle Fork Snoqualmie River Valley. Total elevation gain from PCT trailhead is 2,400 feet.

Views of the surrounding peaks are frequent on the way to Commonwealth Basin.

Directions

From Seattle, drive east on I-90 to Exit 52/West Summit. Turn left at the exit ramp, pass under the freeway, and take the first right into the PCT-North parking area. The road forks—take the right fork to the main parking lot for hikers. The lot to the left is intended for horse trailers. The trail starts at the east end of the parking lot.

Information and Contact

This trail is accessible mid-June–October and is open to hikers and leashed dogs. A federal Northwest Forest Pass is required to park here. For a map of Mount Baker–Snoqualmie National Forest, contact the Outdoor Recreation Information Center at the downtown Seattle REI. For topographic maps, ask Green Trails for No. 207, Snoqualmie Pass, or ask the USGS for Snoqualmie Pass. For more information, contact Mount Baker–Snoqualmie National Forest, North Bend Ranger Station, 42404 Southeast North Bend Way, North Bend, WA 98045, 425/888-1421.

17 KENDALL KATWALK

in the Alpine Lakes Wilderness of Mount Baker–Snoqualmie
National Forest

Level: Moderate/Strenuous	Total Distance: 13.0 miles
Hiking Time: 7 hours	Elevation Gain: 3,000 feet

Summary: Climbing out of old forest into subalpine splendor, this hike visits the best-known stretch of Pacific Crest Trail in Washington.

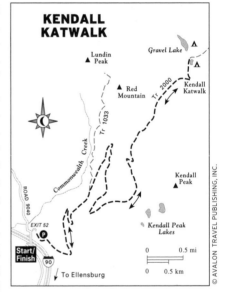

Without a doubt, Kendall Katwalk is one of the most unforgettable and exciting stretches of the 2,600-mile-long Pacific Crest Trail. The Katwalk is a short section of the PCT that encounters a nearly vertical granite wall on the side of Kendall Peak. With a little ingenuity and even more dynamite, trail engineers blasted a 100-yard stretch of trail into the cliff. Named Kendall Katwalk, it's now famous across the country. The rest of the hike isn't half bad either. Climbing out of an old-growth forest, the PCT offers alpine scenery and incredible views of the surrounding mountains. The whole adventure is best capped off with a much-deserved swim in Ridge or Gravel Lake.

The PCT leaves Snoqualmie Pass and quickly begins the ascent to the high country. Much of the hike to Kendall Katwalk is a steady, moderate incline—the length of the hike is more challenging than the ascent. Well-maintained and -graded, the trail passes underfoot quickly in a forest of large Douglas firs and hemlocks. Enjoy the cool shade while it lasts—the latter half of the hike demands sunscreen on sunny days. If you're hiking with a four-legged companion, take note that there are several streams along the first half of the hike, with the last dependable water at 3.5 miles. Beyond, the trail is hot and exposed until Ridge Lake. Be sure to carry plenty of water, not only for yourself but for your dog as well.

© SCOTT LEONARD

Kendall Katwalk is a popular stretch of the Pacific Crest Trail.

The trail makes a slight drop to the first and only junction of the hike with Commonwealth Basin Trail (2.5 miles). Stay to the right on PCT and resume climbing through the forest. Completing a long switchback, the trail reaches a ridge and turns north to traverse a large, open boulder field (4.2 miles). From here on, the trail cuts through meadows where the views are outstanding. A map is highly recommended for identifying the many peaks.

The PCT reaches Kendall Katwalk (5.5 miles) at a gap in the ridge. Although the trail is plenty wide, watch your step; Silver Creek Valley is a good 1,200-foot drop. This beautiful spot deserves all the attention it receives. Countless peaks line the horizon to the east and west. Many hikers have lunch here and call it a day, but hiking a bit farther is recommended. Ridge and Gravel Lakes (6.5 miles) are a short trip beyond the Katwalk. Sitting on opposite sides of a wide saddle, the large lakes are excellent swimming holes and also attract a fair number of fishing poles. There are numerous campsites around the lake for those interested in an overnight excursion.

Directions

From Seattle, drive east on I-90 to Exit 52/West Summit. Turn left at the exit ramp, pass under the freeway, and take the first right into the PCT-North parking area. The road forks—take the right fork to the main parking lot for hikers. The lot to the left is intended for horse trailers. The trail starts at the east end of the parking lot.

Information and Contact

This trail is accessible mid-June–September and is open to hikers and leashed dogs. A federal Northwest Forest Pass is required to park here. For a map of Mount Baker–Snoqualmie National Forest, contact the Outdoor Recreation Information Center at the downtown Seattle REI. For topographic maps, ask Green Trails for No. 207, Snoqualmie Pass, or ask the USGS for Snoqualmie Pass and Chikamin Peak. For more information, contact Mount Baker–Snoqualmie National Forest, North Bend Ranger Station, 42404 Southeast North Bend Way, North Bend, WA 98045, 425/888-1421.

18 GOLD CREEK TRAIL

in the Alpine Lakes Wilderness of Wenatchee National Forest

Level: Easy

Hiking Time: 5 hours

Total Distance: 8.6 miles

Elevation Gain: 300 feet

Summary: An easy valley hike beside a cool stream that is perfect for families.

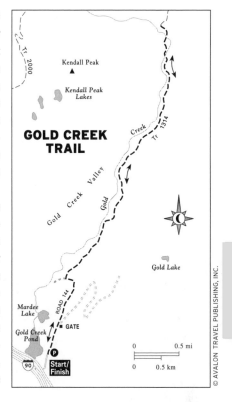

Unlike most other trails in the I-90 corridor, Gold Creek Trail is an easy hike up a dramatic valley. Located just east of Snoqualmie Pass, the gentle trail is a perfect trip for families with kids. There is little elevation gain as the trail ventures four miles through shady forest along Gold Creek. A reroute of the trailhead added 1.3 miles to the hike. Regardless, Gold Creek is still a quiet and pleasant outing.

Because Gold Creek Trail does not summit a big peak or visit a well-known lake, the trail sees a fraction of the heavy use that plagues other I-90 trails. Still, there is drama to be found on this trail. The forest frequently breaks for avalanche chutes and resulting views. The rocky ridges and peaks bordering Gold Creek Valley are a spectacle in their own right. This is an excellent snowshoe route in the winter.

The new trailhead is now at Gold Creek Pond and requires some road hiking to reach the old trailhead. To start the hike, follow Gold Creek Pond Trail around the east side of the pond. A side trail (0.2 mile) leads up to Forest Service Road 144. Hike the road to the old trailhead (1.3 miles). To bike this stretch, pass through the gate on Road 144 immediately before the parking lot and bike the road to the trailhead.

From the signed old trailhead, Gold Creek Trail ventures through shady forest. The trail gains just 300 feet of elevation in the next three miles, all on well-maintained tread, making it accessible by hikers of all abilities. The route frequently encounters open, brushy avalanche chutes where the views are the best. The creekbed makes a nice place for a break (2.0 miles).

On even the hottest summer days, this hike is relatively cool. Sunburn is rarely a problem with the shady canopy. After entering the wilderness (2.3 miles), the trail gently wanders up the valley through stands of large timber. The hike described here ends when the trail requires a crossing of Gold Creek (4.3 miles). There is no bridge here, and a shin-deep fording is required. This is often one of the first trails in the area to be snow-free, making it a great choice in May.

Options

Gold Creek Trail provides access to a pair of remote high-country lakes, Alaska and Joe Lakes. Alaska Lake is a tough climb, while the trail to Joe Lake is downright nasty and not recommended. Although both lakes are more easily accessed via the PCT from Snoqualmie Pass, Gold Creek Trail is the traditional route to Alaska Lake. From where the main trail meets Gold Creek at the end of the above description, ford the creek—a wet but easy endeavor—and continue the gentle hike up-valley. The trail fords Silver Creek (4.7 miles) and continues to a discreet and unsigned junction for Alaska Lake (5.3 miles). The junction is located in the forest immediately before breaking out into open

© CHRIS DUVAL

a view of Gold Creek from the trail

marshland. Turn left and ruthlessly climb 1,100 feet in one mile to the lake (6.3 miles total). A map is indispensable for this option.

Directions

From Seattle, drive east on I-90 to Exit 54/Hyak. Turn left and drive 0.2 mile to Forest Service Road 4832 (signed Gold Creek). Turn right and drive one mile to Forest Service Road 144. Turn left and drive 0.3 mile to the paved parking lot and signed Gold Creek Pond trailhead.

Information and Contact

This trail is accessible April–November and is open to hikers, leashed dogs, and mountain bikes (up to the old trailhead only). A federal Northwest Forest Pass is required to park here. For a map of Mount Baker–Snoqualmie National Forest, contact the Outdoor Recreation Information Center at the downtown Seattle REI. For topographic maps, ask Green Trails for No. 207, Snoqualmie Pass, or ask the USGS for Chikamin Peak. Located in Wenatchee National Forest, the trail is managed by the North Bend Ranger District of Mount Baker–Snoqualmie National Forest. For more information, contact Mount Baker–Snoqualmie National Forest, North Bend Ranger Station, 42404 Southeast North Bend Way, North Bend, WA 98045, 425/888-1421.

19 MARGARET LAKE
in the Alpine Lakes Wilderness of Wenatchee National Forest

Level: Moderate

Hiking Time: 4 hours

Total Distance: 6.2 miles

Elevation Gain: 2,200 feet

Summary: A steep, exposed climb with views to Margaret Lake, nestled in Rampart Ridge.

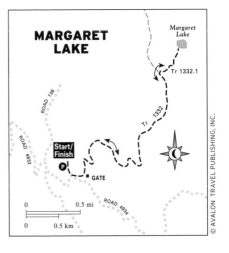

You'd never guess from the jumble of cars at the trailhead that this trail is a steep one or that it endures a hot stretch of hiking along a road and in a clear-cut for the first mile. Of course, the parking lot services several destinations, so the crowd at Margaret Lake isn't as large as it may seem. In spite of the challenges, Margaret Lake is worth the effort. This is a great hike just 70 minutes from Seattle. The hike to Margaret Lake is a companion hike to Lake Lillian (see next listing)—the two share Rampart Ridge Trail for the first 2.6 miles.

The route to Margaret Lake is one of constant elevation change, climbing strenuously to the ridgeline on Rampart Ridge Trail before quickly dropping to the lake on Margaret Lake Trail. Making use of old logging roads and constructed trail, the way to Margaret Lake can be confusing. From the signed parking lot on Forest Service Road 4934, hike uphill on that gravel road 100 yards to the gated road on the left, signed "Trail." From here, hike to a very old road on the left (0.6 mile), marked by cairns. Just 25 yards down this old road is the beginning of real trail, signed "Trail" and climbing to the right.

This narrow trail is Rampart Ridge Trail and zigzags up through an old clear-cut. On hot summer days, the sun beats down on hikers and makes the first mile seem at least twice the distance. Sunscreen and plenty of water are important items to pack even on cool, cloudy days. As unpleasant as clear-cuts may be, this one reveals great views of Mount Rainier, surprisingly big to the south. After crossing an old logging road (1.2 miles), Rampart Ridge

Trail enters cool, old-growth forest of fir and hemlock, a welcome respite from the blazing sun.

Rampart Ridge Trail finally reaches the ridgeline and the Margaret Lake Trail junction (2.6 miles). Head to the right and down Margaret Lake Trail, enjoying views of Chikamin Ridge and Three Queens Peaks. The lake (3.1 miles) is surrounded by a beautiful subalpine meadow mixed with trees, providing shady spots around the lake for lunch. As with most high-country lakes in the area, this one is perfect for a summer swim. Several campsites ring the lake for hikers interested in a quick and easy overnight backpacking getaway.

reaching the crest of Rampart Ridge and looking down to Margaret Lake

Directions

From Seattle, drive east on I-90 to Exit 54/Hyak. Turn left and drive 0.3 mile to Forest Service Road 4832. Turn right and drive five miles to Forest Service Road 4934. Turn left and drive 0.5 mile to the parking area. The signed trailhead is a short walk up Forest Service Road 4934 behind a gated road.

Information and Contact

This trail is accessible June–October and is open to hikers and leashed dogs. A federal Northwest Forest Pass is not required to park here. For a map of Wenatchee National Forest, contact the Outdoor Recreation Information Center at the downtown Seattle REI. For topographic maps, ask Green Trails for No. 207, Snoqualmie Pass, or ask the USGS for Chikamin Peak and Stampede Pass. For more information, contact Wenatchee National Forest, Cle Elum Ranger Station, 803 West 2nd Street, Cle Elum, WA 98922, 509/852-1100.

20 LAKE LILLIAN

in the Alpine Lakes Wilderness of Wenatchee National Forest

Level: Moderate/Strenuous

Hiking Time: 6 hours

Total Distance: 9.2 miles

Elevation Gain: 2,600 feet

Summary: Out of a clear-cut and into old-growth forest, this trail is a challenging hike encompassing three great subalpine lakes.

Lake Lillian is the largest in a series of subalpine lakes nestled along the southern arm of Rampart Ridge. With the craggy buttes of the ridge jutting into the sky above the clear blue lake, this challenging trek is not to be overlooked. As an added bonus, in making its way to Lake Lillian, Rampart Ridge Trail takes time to pass Twin Lakes, a pair of beauties located in a peaceful setting. Despite a rough start along a logging road, passing through a clear-cut, and requiring a good deal of climbing, Rampart Ridge Trail to Lake Lillian is an excellent hike.

The route to Lake Lillian is one of almost constant elevation change, climbing strenuously to the ridgeline and quickly dropping to Twin Lakes, before making a series of strenuous climbs and drops. Making use of old logging roads and constructed trail, the first two miles to Lake Lillian, on Rampart Ridge Trail, can be confusing. From the signed parking lot on Forest Service Road 4934, hike uphill on that gravel road 100 yards to the gated and signed road on the left. From here, hike to a very old road on the left side (0.6 mile), marked by cairns. Just 25 yards down this old road is the beginning of real trail, simply signed as "Trail" and climbing to the right.

This narrow trail is Rampart Ridge Trail and switchbacks through an old clear-cut. On hot summer days, the sun beats down on hikers—don't forget to pack sunscreen and plenty of water, even on cool days. To help with the tax-

views of peaks on the way to Lake Lillian

ing climb are grand views of Mount Rainier to the south. After crossing an old logging road (1.2 miles), the trail enters cool, old-growth forest of fir and hemlock, a welcome respite from the blazing sun.

Rampart Ridge Trail finally reaches the ridgeline and the Margaret Lake Trail junction (2.6 miles). Stay to the left, as Rampart Ridge Trail begins to even out and run the ridge, passing just below Mount Margaret (3.0 miles). The trail next drops rapidly to Twin Lakes (3.8 miles), a pair of beautiful lakes surrounded by subalpine meadow. This is an excellent place for tired or time-constrained hikers to turn back. By themselves, Twin Lakes are a great destination.

Continuing to Lillian Lake, Rampart Ridge Trail makes a series of strenuous drops and climbs. Some sections are nearly a scramble, with rocks and roots offering a much-needed helping hand. The effort pays off, as the trail reaches the large basin holding Lake Lillian (4.6 miles). Set beneath the rocky crags of Rampart Ridge, the lake offers an inviting swim on hot summer days. With open meadows ringing the lake, wildflowers add an extra element of beauty in early July.

Options

Several campsites ring the lake for those interested in an overnight backpacking trip. For hikers with extra energy, an obvious but unofficial extension of Rampart Ridge Trail runs from the back side of Lake Lillian to the peaks of Rampart Ridge, high above the lake.

Directions

From Seattle, drive east on I-90 to Exit 54/Hyak. Turn left and drive 0.3 mile to Forest Service Road 4832. Turn right and drive five miles to Forest Service Road 4934. Turn left and drive 0.5 mile to the parking area. The signed trailhead is a short walk up Forest Service Road 4934 behind a gated road.

Information and Contact

This trail is accessible mid-June–mid-October and is open to hikers and leashed dogs. A federal Northwest Forest Pass is not required to park here. For a map of Wenatchee National Forest, contact the Outdoor Recreation Information Center at the downtown Seattle REI. For topographic maps, ask Green Trails for No. 207, Snoqualmie Pass, or ask the USGS for Chikamin Peak and Stampede Pass. For more information, contact Wenatchee National Forest, Cle Elum Ranger Station, 803 West 2nd Street, Cle Elum, WA 98922, 509/852-1100.

21 RACHEL LAKE

in the Alpine Lakes Wilderness of Wenatchee National Forest

Level: Moderate

Total Distance: 8.0 miles

Hiking Time: 4 hours

Elevation Gain: 2,000 feet

Summary: A heavily traveled route to a scenic lake on the drier eastern side of Alpine Lakes Wilderness.

Rachel Lake is one of the most popular destinations along the I-90 corridor. Crowds are a given on just about any day of the week, a testament to the beauty of the lake. From forests of big trees to meadows with big views, there's no shortage of appeal to this hike. When such a great hike is this easy to access, it's no wonder the trail is popular. For those with a sense of adventure, the hike has a great option for an extension with the hike to Rampart Ridge above Rachel Lake.

Be forewarned that the hike to Rachel Lake is more demanding than it might seem on paper. The final mile to the lake is a steep and physically challenging gain of 1,400 feet. So, despite the popularity of the trail, it isn't for kids. The trail is especially hot on sunny summer days. Packing plenty of water and trail food is a good idea.

The first three miles of Rachel Lake Trail are relatively flat and pass quickly. This section parallels Box Canyon Creek through forest and occasional avalanche chutes, where colorful fireweed dominates the openings. Look north to the towering peaks of Hi Box Mountain. At 2.7 miles, the trail gets mean and climbs steeply up the headwall of the canyon. This is a difficult section, not only for the incline but also due to the poor tread—rocky, rooty, and lacking real design, it's a bear of a stretch.

The views begin to appear as you enter the subalpine forest of the high country, where the trail levels out and reaches the shores of Rachel Lake (3.7 miles). There are many spots for a picnic or a campsite scattered around the lake. Naturally, the lake is ideal for a swim after the hot climb. Rachel Lake and Rampart Ridge have seen a lot of use, with denuded areas abounding—follow Leave No Trace practices in all lake basins.

Options

Rampart Ridge offers a pair of great options for those who haven't tired on the way to Rachel Lake. From the lakeshore, Rachel Lake Trail quickly climbs 600 feet to a T intersection on Rampart Ridge (4.3 miles). This is true parkland—acres of meadows with patches of subalpine fir and mountain hemlock. Small lakes and tarns are scattered about. The wildflowers are prolific in the early summer. Oh, and the views aren't bad either. From the intersection, one trail turns left (south) and drops slightly to Rampart Lakes (1.0 mile from the intersection). The other fork runs north along the ridge to tiny Lila Lake (0.7 mile from the intersection).

Directions

From Seattle, drive east on I-90 to Exit 62. Turn left on Kachess Lake Road and drive 5.5 miles to Forest Service Road 4930. Turn right and drive 3.5 miles to the trailhead at road's end.

Information and Contact

This trail is accessible June–October and is open to hikers and leashed dogs. A federal Northwest Forest Pass is required to park here. A free wilderness permit is also required to hike here and is available at the trailhead. For a map of Wenatchee National Forest, contact the Outdoor Recreation Information Center at the downtown Seattle REI. For topographic maps, ask Green Trails for No. 207, Snoqualmie Pass, or ask the USGS for Chikamin Peak. For more information, contact Wenatchee National Forest, Cle Elum Ranger District, 803 West 2nd Street, Cle Elum, WA 98922, 509/852-1100.

MOUNT RAINIER

© SCOTT LEONARD

BEST HIKES

Easily the Northwest's tallest point (by more than 2,000 feet), Mount Rainier never seems to be far from view. At 14,411 feet, the towering mass of The Mountain looms over life in Puget Sound, western Washington, and a good chunk of the east side as well. From old-growth forest to alpine meadows, from icy glaciers to milky white rivers, Mount Rainier has it all. A total of 26 glaciers grace the slopes of Takhoma (which, in Puyallup, means "breast of the milk-white waters"). These glistening masses of ice give birth to opalescent rivers flowing in every direction.

There are several points of access to one of the nation's most famous and heavily visited national parks: The easiest park access from Seattle is in the northwest corner at Carbon River and Mowich Lake. The hikes included in this chapter offer a diverse sampling of what Mount Rainier has to offer. All reachable within two hours or less from Seattle, the hikes pass along the northwestern and northeastern corners of the national park and are comfortably accomplished in one day.

Greenwater Lakes Trail is a short, level hike that passes through a forest of giant Douglas Fir and Western Hemlock on the way to a pair of small lakes, while Green Lake Trail, inside the national park, features some of the park's biggest firs and an outstanding waterfall on Ranger Creek. Most dramatic of all the big-tree hikes is Carbon River, a hike through old growth and over the river on an unforgettable suspension bridge, ending at the snout of a glacier.

A number of hikes feature the glorious meadows of the region. Starting at Mowich Lake, Spray Park Trail is one of Mount Rainier's finest, climbing up to acres of wildflower meadows at the mountain's base. And the easy hike to Tolmie Peak is a good option for families.

Finally, several hikes included here are not within the national park. The hikes to Noble Knob and Bear Gap are located near the Cascade Crest and have a distinctive feel — they are noticeably drier, marking the beginning of the transition to the dry eastside of the state. The moderate hike to the bald summit of Noble Knob offers views in every direction, from the Olympics to the North Cascades and down to Mount Rainier. And the loop hike to Bear Gap traverses the beloved Pacific Crest Trail.

The views and meadows along these hikes seem to never end, making a day spent hiking on Mount Rainier an unforgettable adventure.

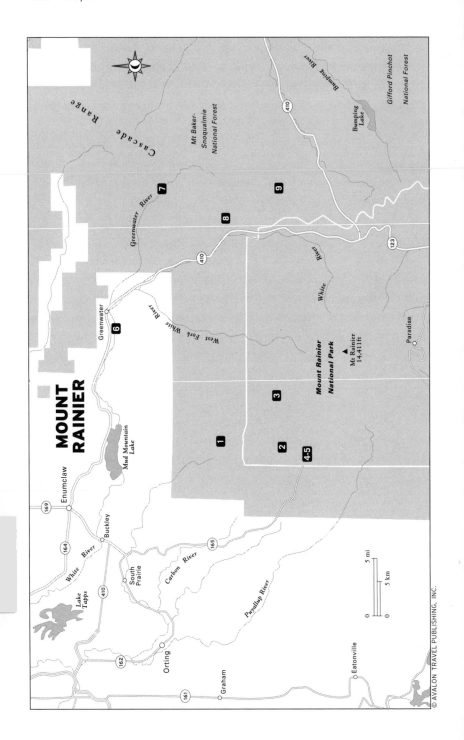

Mount Rainier Hikes

1 SUMMIT LAKE

in the Clearwater Wilderness of Mount Baker-Snoqualmie National Forest

Level: Easy/Moderate

Hiking Time: 3 hours

Total Distance: 4.8 miles

Elevation Gain: 1,100 feet

Summary: A nice, short hike into subalpine meadows to visit the Clearwater Wilderness's largest lake.

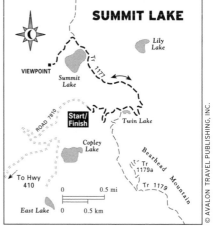

If you've never heard of the Clearwater, don't be surprised. It's easily overshadowed by its big sister to the south, Mount Rainier National Park. The hike to Summit Lake enjoys all the marvelous views of The Mountain with none of the extra crowds or cost of a trip inside the national park. This hike is great in July, when wildflowers are in full bloom in the lake basin.

Summit Lake, which shares a trailhead with Bearhead Mountain, is the easier of the two hikes (see *Options*) but still features plenty of nice views. Beginning from the trailhead, the two destinations share Summit Lake Trail as it climbs through an old clear-cut. The trail crosses Twin Creek twice, the second time at the outlet of the small lake (0.8 mile). Here, the trail splits—stay to the left on Summit Lake Trail.

Summit Lake Trail continues climbing through old forest protected by the wilderness designation, which is a quasi extension of the national park. A good thing, too, because at this high altitude, mountain hemlock and subalpine fir take centuries to reach the relatively modest size of these trees. The trail finally breaks out of the forest when it reaches the lake basin nestled into the side of the ridge (2.4 miles).

Views of Mount Rainier are outstanding from the lakeshore. If you're willing to brave some cold water, this is a great swimming hole. Wildflowers arrive in July while huckleberries wait until late August. A small path rings the lake and encounters several campsites. Expect a pesky amount of bugs in early summer.

Options

If you have an itch to bag a peak and get some more views, you have two options. The easiest option is located at Summit Lake. Stay on the main trail as it passes the lake. An obvious path scrambles to the top of the small, unnamed peak on the lake's western side. This option is a total of three miles.

The other option is a summit of Bearhead Mountain, a 1,700-foot climb in three miles to the top of the long, rocky peak. From Twin Lake (0.8 mile), turn right onto Carbon Trail and hike south. This route junctions with Bearhead Mountain Trail (2.2 miles). Turn left and scramble steeply to the summit at 6,089 feet (3.0 miles).

Directions

From Seattle, drive east on I-90 to I-405. Turn south on I-405 and drive to Exit 4/Highway 169. Drive south on Highway 169 25 miles to Enumclaw. Follow signs for Highway 410 West. Turn west on Highway 410 and drive four miles to Highway 165 in the town of Buckley. Turn left (south) and drive 10 miles, through the towns of Wilkeson and Carbonado, to Carbon River Road at a signed fork in the road. Veer left and drive 7.5 miles to Cayada Creek Road (Forest Service Road 7810). Turn left and drive seven miles to the trailhead at road's end.

Information and Contact

This trail is accessible mid-June–September and is open to hikers, leashed dogs, and horses. A federal Northwest Forest Pass is required to park here. For a map of Mount Baker–Snoqualmie National Forest, contact the Outdoor Recreation Information Center at the downtown Seattle REI. For topographic maps, ask Green Trails for No. 237, Enumclaw, or ask the USGS for Bearhead Mountain. For more information, contact Mount Baker–Snoqualmie National Forest, Enumclaw Ranger Station, 450 Roosevelt Avenue East, Enumclaw, WA 98022, 360/825-6585.

2 GREEN LAKE TRAIL

BEST

Mount Rainier National Park

Level: Easy/Moderate

Total Distance: 3.4 miles

Hiking Time: 2 hours

Elevation Gain: 1,200 feet

Summary: A short but appreciable climb to beautiful Green Lake with a stop by Ranger Falls along the way.

Green Lake Trail throws conventional wisdom out the window. Why do you need acres of meadow or dozens of bug bites to have a good time? Not on Green Lake Trail. Why do you need to bag lofty peaks and contract a nasty case of sunburn to call it a great day? Nope, not on Green Lake Trail. This casual hike instead explores superb old-growth forest on its way to one of Rainier's few lakes not stashed away up in the subalpine heights. The trail also passes Ranger Falls, a dandy of a cascade. Keep in mind that the Carbon River Valley is a popular destination. Summer weekends are the worst, but expect company on the trail any day.

Green Lake Trail leaves Carbon River Road and begins climbing up the forested hillside. The forest here is remarkably green and lush, with ferns and mosses growing on anything that will sit still. The old-growth timber is as impressive as any in the park. Some Douglas firs are more than 800 years old. The Carbon River Valley receives more rainfall than any other part of the park. In spite of that fact, the trail tread is in good condition and the route is regularly brushed. Many improvements have been made to the tread using native cedar.

The halfway point is marked by Ranger Falls (0.9 mile), the ideal time and place for a break. The falls are just off the trail to the left and are accessed by a short side trail that leads to a great viewpoint. In spring, snowmelt pours over the fall and creates a shower of mist. This is one place where even a sunny day may call for rain gear.

From Ranger Falls, Green Lake Trail continues climbing toward the lake.

Green Lake Trail passes through some of Mount Rainier National Park's largest forests.

You know you're approaching Green Lake when the trail briefly levels out and crosses Ranger Creek on a small footbridge (1.6 miles). Beyond, it drops slightly to the lakeshore. A small clearing makes a good place to eat lunch. Just don't feed the chipmunks or camp robbers (gray jays)—they're already aggressive enough here. Green Lake is surrounded by forest with steep cliffs above. Up the narrow valley is a nice view of Tolmie Peak and its lookout.

Directions

From Seattle, drive east on I-90 to I-405. Turn south on I-405 and drive to Exit 4/Highway 169. Drive south on Highway 169 25 miles to Enumclaw. Follow signs for Highway 410 West. Turn west on Highway 410 and drive four miles to Highway 165 in the town of Buckley. Turn left (south) and drive 10 miles, through the towns of Wilkeson and Carbonado, to Carbon River Road at a signed fork in the road. Veer left and drive 11 miles to the signed parking area (on the left) and trailhead (on the right).

Information and Contact

This trail is accessible May–October and is open to hikers only—dogs are not allowed. A National Park Pass is required to park here. Passes can be purchased at the Carbon River Guard Station, located at the park boundary on Carbon River Road. For a map of Mount Rainier National Park, contact the Outdoor Recreation Information Center at the downtown Seattle REI. For topographic maps, ask Green Trails for No. 269, Mount Rainier West, or ask the USGS for Mowich Lake. For more information, contact Mount Rainier National Park, Wilkeson Wilderness Information Center, P.O. Box 423, Wilkeson, WA 98396, 360/829-5127.

3 CARBON GLACIER
Mount Rainier National Park

Level: Easy/Moderate

Hiking Time: 4 hours

Total Distance: 7.0 miles

Elevation Gain: 1,300 feet

Summary: A spectacular sampling of Mount Rainier, this hike passes waterfalls, crosses an enormous suspension bridge, and reaches the largest glacier in the lower 48 states.

The hike to Carbon Glacier follows the most scenic stretch of valley on the famed Wonderland Trail. Within the old-growth forest of the Carbon Valley, Wonderland Trail passes several waterfalls before coming face-to-face with one of America's biggest glaciers. The highlight of the journey for many isn't the glacier—it's the gut-wrenching walk across the colossal suspension bridge spanning the river With so many great things to see, this is the best day hike in Mount Rainier National Park.

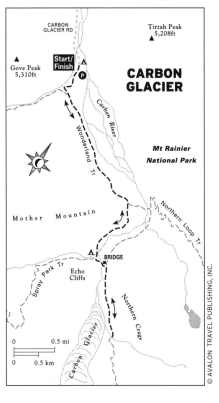

This is a great trail for hikers of all experience levels. The elevation gain is evenly spread along the route and kids love crossing the suspension bridge. However, don't expect solitude along this hike. The route is a segment of the popular Wonderland and Northern Loop Trails. Weekdays in the spring and fall are good times to find the trail relatively vacant.

The hike leaves the parking lot at Ipsut Creek Campground and quickly encounters a side trail on the right to Ipsut Falls (0.1 mile). Be sure to check out this quick detour to the large falls. The main trail follows the Carbon River and reaches a junction with the Wonderland Trail (0.3 mile). Stay left on the Wonderland Trail as it parallels the river and heads up the valley. The Carbon River's turbid water looks incredibly dirty, but, in fact, it's

the large suspension bridge spanning the Carbon River, just below the glacier

filled with rock flour, the product of the glacier grinding up and eroding the mountain.

The Wonderland Trail leaves the river and reaches a junction for the southern crossing (1.9 miles), an alternate route (see *Options*). Stay on the Wonderland Trail as it again encounters the river and a wide riverbed of boulders and glacial moraine. Carbon River Camp (2.8 miles) is located along Cataract Creek where it cascades over large boulders beside the trail.

The Wonderland Trail crosses the Carbon River on a large suspension bridge (3.0 miles) spanning more than 200 feet. Even the sturdiest of hikers will be knocking knees as they peer down through the boards to the raging river 40 feet below. At the east end of the bridge, turn right and climb to the snout of Carbon Glacier (3.5 miles).

Acting like a giant bulldozer and covered in rocks and dirt, the end of the glacier is slowly pushing chunks of the mountain down the slope. The Carbon Glacier is the largest in the lower 48 states, both in depth (700 feet thick in some places) and volume. It is also the lowest glacier, with its terminus at just 3,600 feet of elevation. Although the glacier looks benign, appearances are deceiving. Small rock slides occur frequently and are extremely dangerous. The glacier is best viewed from the trail.

Options

Experienced and adventure-seeking hikers can add a small loop to this hike. The Northern Loop Trail parallels the Carbon River on the eastern banks.

From the east end of the suspension bridge, hike south 1.1 miles on the Northern Loop Trail to a signed junction. Turn left on an unnamed connector trail and cross the river back to the Wonderland Trail. This crossing is sketchy and regularly washes out. Check with the ranger at the guard station on the road in to see if this south crossing is passable.

Directions

From Seattle, drive east on I-90 to I-405. Turn south on I-405 and drive to Exit 4/Highway 169. Drive south on Highway 169 25 miles to Enumclaw. Follow signs for Highway 410 West. Turn west on Highway 410 and drive four miles to Highway 165 in the town of Buckley. Turn left (south) and drive 10 miles, through the towns of Wilkeson and Carbonado, to Carbon River Road at a signed fork in the road. Veer left and drive 13 miles to the signed parking area at Ipsut Creek Campground at the end of the road. The signed trailhead is at the back of the parking lot.

Information and Contact

This trail is accessible mid-May–October and is open to hikers only—dogs are not allowed. A National Park Pass is required to park here. Passes can be purchased at the Carbon River Guard Station, located at the park boundary on Carbon River Road. For a map of Mount Rainier National Park, contact the Outdoor Recreation Information Center at the downtown Seattle REI. For topographic maps, ask Green Trails for No. 269, Mount Rainier West, or ask the USGS for Mowich Lake. For more information, contact Mount Rainier National Park, Wilkeson Wilderness Information Center, P.O. Box 423, Wilkeson, WA 98396, 360/829-5127.

4 TOLMIE PEAK   BEST 🅒
Mount Rainier National Park

🚹 🦌 🏕 🛶 👫 ⛷

Level: Moderate   **Total Distance:** 6.4 miles

Hiking Time: 3.5 hours   **Elevation Gain:** 1,100 feet

Summary: An easy hike from one high lake to another before climbing quickly to a rustic fire lookout soaked in views.

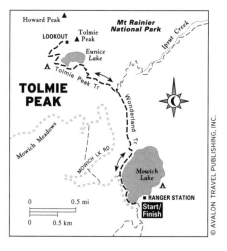

Tolmie Peak is one of Mount Rainier's best day hikes. Traveling along the shores of two subalpine lakes and then shooting skyward to a fire lookout, the trail rarely disappoints. Throughout the hike, Mount Rainier looms dramatically nearby. The view from the fire lookout is spectacular and one of my favorites in Washington. The final ascent to the lookout is the only difficult part of the hike. If the steep climb doesn't sound appealing, the meadows of Eunice Lake are a great turnaround point.

Keep in mind that the hike is located in the northwest corner of the national park. With the long, bumpy access road, it takes nearly two hours to reach the trailhead. Being a bit remote, the area doesn't receive the hordes of people that Paradise or Sunrise Visitors Centers attract. Still, expect company on the trail. Mowich Lake is a popular send-off point for the Wonderland Trail and day hikes, especially this one.

The hike begins on the Wonderland Trail. From the parking lot nearest the walk-in campground, the unsigned trail drops to the lakeshore and winds around the western shore clockwise. Leaving the lake (0.7 mile), the Wonderland Trail contours the side of a small forested ridge to Ipsut Pass and a junction with Tolmie Peak Trail (1.5 miles). Take a left on Tolmie Peak Trail as the Wonderland Trail crosses the pass and drops down along Ipsut Creek.

Tolmie Peak Trail continues along the ridge before several quick but easy switchbacks rise to Eunice Lake (2.3 miles). Surrounded by meadows and small clusters of trees, the lake is picturesque with Mount Rainier in the background. Wildflowers are in full bloom in July. This subalpine environment is very fragile—help take care of it by sticking to the main trail at all times. The gain in elevation to Eunice Lake is just 500 feet, so it makes for a shorter, much easier option.

The final stretch of Tolmie Peak Trail climbs sharply along the forested slope to the summit (3.2 miles). The lookout is staffed occasionally during the summer. The views extend for miles in every direction, from The Mountain up to the North Cascades and out west to the Olympics. When it comes to bang for the buck, Tolmie is a great deal.

Directions

From Seattle, drive east on I-90 to I-405. Turn south on I-405 and drive to Exit 4/Highway 169. Drive south on Highway 169 25 miles to Enumclaw. Follow signs for Highway 410 West. Turn west on Highway 410 and drive four miles to Highway 165 in the town of Buckley. Turn left (south) and drive five miles to the Wilkeson Wilderness Information Center, where you can purchase a parking pass. From Wilkeson, continue driving on Highway 165 five miles to a signed fork in the road. Veer right and drive 16 miles to the signed parking area at Mowich Lake at the end of the road. The signed trailhead drops down to the lake.

Information and Contact

This trail is accessible June–October and is open to hikers only—dogs are not allowed. A National Park Pass is required to park here. Passes can be purchased at the Wilkeson Wilderness Information Center in the town of Wilkeson. For a map of Mount Rainier National Park, contact the Outdoor Recreation Information Center at the downtown Seattle REI. For topographic maps, ask Green Trails for No. 269, Mount Rainier West, or ask the USGS for Mowich Lake and Golden Lakes. For more information, contact Mount Rainier National Park, Wilkeson Wilderness Information Center, P.O. Box 423, Wilkeson, WA 98396, 360/829-5127.

5 SPRAY PARK

BEST ☾

Mount Rainier National Park

Level: Moderate

Total Distance: 8.4 miles

Hiking Time: 5 hours

Elevation Gain: 2,100 feet

Summary: An outstanding hike to one of Mount Rainier's best meadows, with views and waterfalls to boot.

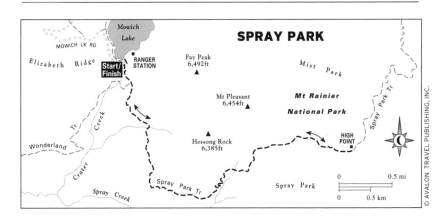

You don't need to hike the nearly 100 miles of Wonderland Trail to enjoy the splendor of Mount Rainier's enormous meadows. Spray Park is one of The Mountain's finest, nestled on its northwest slopes. The rocky meadows are chock-full of views and flowers. The hike there isn't half bad, either. Eagle Cliff offers a stomach-crunching view out over the Mowich Valley, and Spray Falls are gorgeous. Hands down, the hike to Spray Park is an exceptional time on the slopes of Washington's favorite icon.

Spray Park is located in the northwest corner of Mount Rainier National Park. Accessing the trailhead requires driving on a long, bumpy access road– the trailhead is a good two-hour drive from Seattle. And although this area is remote, it is still popular in the summer–expect company on the trail. With that said, the hike to Spray Park is worth the drive and crowds.

From Mowich Lake's walk-in campground, the Wonderland Trail drops down beside Crater Creek to the junction with Spray Park Trail (0.3 mile). Turn left on Spray Park Trail as it contours the forested hillside and crosses Lee Creek (0.8 mile). The trail descends slightly before arriving at Eagle Cliff (1.2 miles) and the first great views of Mount Rainier. Spray Park Trail then climbs to Eagles Roost Camp (2.0 miles) and reaches a short side trail to Spray Falls on the right (2.1 miles). The 10-minute walk to Spray Falls is a must.

Spray Park Trail then gets serious, climbing sharply out of the forest and into the open expanse of Spray Park (3.0 miles). Mount Rainier is so large and looming that it's breathtaking. The meadows catch fire with blooming wildflowers after the winter snow pack melts off, reaching their peak in July. Bear in mind that when wildflowers are out, the mosquitoes likely are too. These subalpine meadows are extremely fragile. Please help protect them by staying on the constructed trail.

Spray Park Trail steadily climbs for a full mile through the meadows of Spray Park to a high ridge at 6,400 feet, the hike's turnaround point (4.2 miles). On even the sunniest of days, be ready for quickly changing weather. Clouds roll in swiftly on Mount Rainier, and the temperature can fluctuate greatly. Cloudy days here are fun too—just be prepared for the unexpected.

Directions

From Seattle, drive east on I-90 to I-405. Turn south on I-405 and drive to Exit 4/Highway 169. Drive south on Highway 169 25 miles to Enumclaw. Follow signs for Highway 410 West. Turn west on Highway 410 and drive four miles to Highway 165 in the town of Buckley. Turn left (south) and drive five miles to the Wilkeson Wilderness Information Center, where you can purchase a parking pass. From Wilkeson, continue driving on Highway 165 five miles to a signed fork in the road. Veer right and drive 16 miles to the signed parking area at Mowich Lake at the end of the road. The signed trailhead is located within the walk-in campground.

Information and Contact

This trail is accessible June–October and is open to hikers only—dogs are not allowed. A National Park Pass is required to park here. Passes can be purchased at the Wilkeson Wilderness Information Center in the town of Wilkeson. For a map of Mount Rainier National Park, contact the Outdoor Recreation Information Center at the downtown Seattle REI. For topographic maps, ask Green Trails for No. 269, Mount Rainier West, or ask the USGS for Mowich Lake. For more information, contact Mount Rainier National Park, Wilkeson Wilderness Information Center, P.O. Box 423, Wilkeson, WA 98396, 360/829-5127.

6 FEDERATION FOREST
Federation Forest State Park

Level: Easy

Total Distance: 6.6 miles

Hiking Time: 3 hours

Elevation Gain: 0 feet

Summary: A quiet walk through old-growth forest.

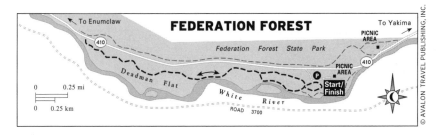

Inconspicuously tucked away on Highway 410 is Federation Forest State Park, home to an outstanding grove of old-growth forest. More than 600 acres of forest are within the park, which is situated along the White River. Federation Forest State Park was made possible by donations from Washington State Federation of Women's Clubs, who sought to conserve the ancient forest. This hike is a quiet ramble through the forest, beginning on a nature loop before heading out on the Naches Trail, one of the few remaining segments of an old pioneer road. The return is along the last half of the nature loop. Unfortunately, there are few views of the river from the trail.

The hike begins at a kiosk, located around the right side of the Interpretive Center. Of the three trails, take the one on the far right, signed West Nature Trail. The trail immediately enters prime old-growth forest. The Douglas firs, hemlocks, and cedars are enormous and tall enough to put a kink in the neck. The forest is a lush green in this area, which receives more than 80 inches of rain each year. Numerous signs are scattered along the trail, offering names of trees and plants.

West Nature Trail reaches a signed junction (0.6 mile). Turn right on Naches Trail, which quickly reaches a kiosk and junction (0.9 mile). Two trails both head toward the river—take the unsigned right fork, which is called Hobbit Trail. This section of trail is notoriously muddy, as the route wanders through a small wetland of skunk cabbage, devil's club, and more big trees.

Hobbit Trail eventually widens and looks like an old roadbed, which it is. This is the old Naches Road, the route followed by early settlers in the mid-1800s.

The trail curves away from the river and ends at Highway 410, the turnaround point. Retrace your steps on Hobbit and Naches Trails until you reach the first junction at the nature loop. Here, turn right on East Nature Loop Trail for a different route back to the original starting point. This hike is perfect for hikers of all ages and abilities.

Directions

From Seattle, drive east on I-90 to I-405. Turn south and drive to Exit 4/ Highway 169. Drive south 25 miles to Enumclaw. Follow signs to Highway 410 and turn east, toward Mount Rainier. Drive 15 miles to the Interpretive Center at Federation Forest State Park, on the right past milepost 41.

Information and Contact

This trail is accessible year-round and is open to hikers and leashed dogs. A $5 day-use fee is required to park here and is payable at the trailhead, or you can get an annual State Parks Pass for $50; contact Washington State Parks and Recreation, 360/902-8500. For topographic maps, ask Green Trails for No. 269, Mount Rainier West, or ask the USGS for Greenwater. For more information, contact Federation Forest State Park, Highway 410 East, Enumclaw, WA 98022, 360/663-2207.

7 GREENWATER TRAIL

BEST ◖

Mount Baker-Snoqualmie National Forest

🦌 🛶 🛷 🐕 👫 🎿

Level: Easy

Total Distance: 4.0 miles

Hiking Time: 2 hours

Elevation Gain: 350 feet

Summary: An easy stroll following the Greenwater River through rocky gorges and exceptional old-growth forest.

A trip along Greenwater Trail is less about Greenwater Lakes than the hike itself. The lakes offer a nice lunch spot and are popular with anglers, but the trip to the lakes is what this hike is all about. Greenwater Trail rambles through outstanding virgin forest as it traces the river to a pair of low-elevation lakes. Along the way, the trail crosses and recrosses the river over several wooden bridges. This easy trip is ideal for hikers of any age or ability.

Greenwater Trail wastes little time before jumping into virgin forest. Al-though logging occurred within this valley, steep slopes prevented the cuts from reaching down to the valley floor and river. The result is a long strip of untouched forest, which this hike never leaves. The trail first crosses the river (0.7 mile) before reaching a beautiful waterfall (1.0 mile). Douglas firs, western red cedars, and western hemlocks show their full potential, growing to enormous sizes.

The route encounters its only ascent as it gently climbs to a view of the river flowing over exposed bedrock (1.4 miles). The trail makes its second crossing of the river (1.6 miles) in a beautiful setting, where the river flows beneath a large mossy cliff. Lower Greenwater Lake, the smaller of the two, is immedi-ately beyond this crossing. Several footpaths lead to picnic or camping sites around the lake.

Continue hiking on Greenwater Trail as it crosses the river two final times be-fore finding Upper Greenwater Lake (2.0 miles). Ringed by hillsides of quiet for-est, the lake is a good place to see wildlife, from woodpeckers and eagles to deer and elk. Fishing is allowed in both lakes, which are slowly and naturally being

filled with sediment. Several campsites can be found along the lakeshore
as the trail wraps around the east side
of Upper Greenwater Lake.

Options

Greenwater Trail also provides access to two backcountry lakes in
the Norse Peak Wilderness. Beyond
Greenwater Lakes, the trail reaches a
signed junction and splits (3.1 miles).
Lost Lake Trail (to the right) climbs
gently through forest and meadows
to its namesake, lying beneath the
rocky ridge of Mutton Mountain (6.0
miles). Greenwater Trail continues
to the left to Echo Lake (6.5 miles).
Both lakes have campsites.

lush and shady trees along Greenwater Trail

Directions

From Seattle, drive east on I-90 to I-405. Turn south and drive to Exit 4/
Highway 169. Drive south 25 miles to Enumclaw. Follow signs to Highway
410 and turn east, toward Mount Rainier. Drive 19 miles to Forest Service
Road 70. Turn left and drive 10 miles to Forest Service Road 7033, signed
Greenwater Trailhead. Turn right—cars park in the lot to the right, the loca-
tion of the signed trailhead.

Information and Contact

This trail is accessible April–November and is open to hikers, leashed dogs,
and horses. A federal Northwest Forest Pass is required to park here. For a
map of Mount Baker–Snoqualmie National Forest, contact the Outdoor Recreation Information Center at the downtown Seattle REI. For topographic
maps, ask Green Trails for No. 239, Lester, or ask the USGS for Noble Knob.
For more information, contact Mount Baker–Snoqualmie National Forest,
Enumclaw Ranger Station, 450 Roosevelt Avenue East, Enumclaw, WA 98022,
360/825-6585.

8 NOBLE KNOB   BEST ☾

Mount Baker-Snoqualmie National Forest

🏕 🦌 🌲 🏞 👫

Level: Easy/Moderate   **Total Distance:** 7.4 miles

Hiking Time: 4 hours   **Elevation Gain:** 1,200 feet

Summary: Starting at a high elevation and ending even higher, Noble Knob Trail is awash in views of rocky ridges and Mount Rainier.

It isn't difficult to imagine what a hike at 6,000 feet is like in this region. Awesome views of Mount Rainier and the North Cascades? Check. Acres of pure meadow bliss? Check. July wildflowers, encounters with elk or coyote, and old forest? Check. A long, taxing climb that seems to never end? Forget about it. Noble Knob Trail starts high and stays there for its duration. That's the beauty of a trailhead at 5,700 feet elevation—trails this great rarely come at such an easy price. This is an excellent hike in Mount Rainier's backyard, a two-hour drive from Seattle.

Noble Knob Trail starts out as single-track trail but soon encounters an old roadbed (0.4 mile), where it continues north (left) on the roadbed's double tracks. The forest is very old here. Alaskan yellow cedars, subalpine fir, and mountain hemlock have grown incredibly large considering the high elevation. It's not long before regular views of Mount Rainier appear to the south through breaks in the forest.

Noble Knob Trail passes open meadows beneath the rock summit of Mutton Mountain (1.0 mile) before climbing to the first junction (1.4 miles). Stay to the right as Noble Knob Trail passes a long section of more great forest on the side of Dalles Ridge. The trail reaches the crest of the ridge (3.0 miles) and makes a steep drop to a saddle between Noble Knob and Dalles Ridge. During this drop, stay right on Noble Knob Trail at the signed junction (3.1 miles).

The saddle is filled with wildflowers in late June and July. Hawks patrol

Map labels: George Lake, Tr 1185, Noble Knob, Lost Lake, **NOBLE KNOB**, Dalles Ridge, Tr 1184, Mutton Mountain, Tr 1196, 0 0.5 mi, 0 0.5 km, ROAD 7174, Start/Finish, To Hwy 410

© AVALON TRAVEL PUBLISHING, INC.

A summer sunset lights up Noble Knob.

the skies above as deer and elk graze the meadows. At the north end of the saddle is an unsigned three-way junction (3.3 miles). The middle trail climbs up the slopes of Noble Knob to the summit (3.7 miles). Although much of the trail climbs gently, this disheartening up and down is a quick 800-foot elevation change.

The summit of Noble Knob is everything one could expect. The panoramic view spans from Mount Rainier out to the Olympics and north to a full spread of the North Cascades. Be prepared for this hike with sunscreen and extra water in the summer—hot, sunny days quickly become exhausting on this trail. On weekdays, the trail is sparsely populated, but on weekends, expect frequent company.

Options
The trailhead is located next to Corral Pass Campground, which is a free stay for hikers with a Northwest Forest Pass. To access the campground, turn right at the fork six miles up Forest Service Road 7145 and drive 0.3 mile.

Directions
From Seattle, drive east on I-90 to I-405. Turn south and drive south to Exit 4/Highway 169. Drive south 25 miles to Enumclaw. Follow signs to Highway 410 and turn east, toward Mount Rainier. Drive 31 miles to signed Forest Service Road 7145, just beyond milepost 56. Turn left and drive six miles on

a very steep, rugged dirt road. The road is regularly maintained and is passable for passenger cars. At six miles, the road forks—turn left for Noble Knob trailhead and parking area. The trailhead is at the end of the parking lot.

Information and Contact

This trail is accessible June–September and is open to hikers, leashed dogs, and horses. A federal Northwest Forest Pass is required to park here. For a map of Mount Baker–Snoqualmie National Forest, contact the Outdoor Recreation Information Center at the downtown Seattle REI. For topographic maps, ask Green Trails for No. 239, Lester, or ask the USGS for Noble Knob. For more information, contact Mount Baker–Snoqualmie National Forest, Enumclaw Ranger Station, 450 Roosevelt Avenue East, Enumclaw, WA 98022, 360/825-6585.

9 BEAR GAP TO BULLION BASIN

Mount Baker-Snoqualmie National Forest

Level: Moderate

Total Distance: 7.5 miles

Hiking Time: 4.5 hours

Elevation Gain: 1,800 feet

Summary: This loop hike makes use of the Pacific Crest Trail through an awesome segment east of Mount Rainier.

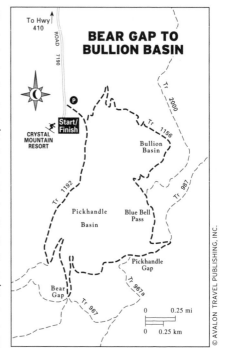

The Pacific Crest Trail is the most well-known trail on the West Coast. Stretching from Mexico up to Canada, the trail rides the crest of the Cascades in Oregon and Washington. Although most of the route lies deep in the backcountry, several beautiful sections are easily accessed; this is one of the best. Due east of Mount Rainier National Park, this loop hike climbs to the PCT as it rambles around Pickhandle Basin. There are plenty of great views, some obvious (Mount Rainier) and some surprising (Mount Adams). Although this day hike is a good two hours from Seattle, it's an excellent hike for the effort. Much of the PCT is in open, exposed meadows. Hot summer days can be especially draining, so sunscreen and extra water are important.

From the trailhead, the signed route climbs to a gravel access road (0.2 mile) for the ski resort, where Silver Spring Trail and Bullion Basin Trail converge at a switchback in the road. Turn right on signed Silver Spring Trail. The trail passes beneath a ski lift and enters the cool forest before making a relentless climb to a signed junction on Elizabeth Creek (2.3 miles). Head to the left, toward the PCT, as the trail ascends to Bear Gap (3.0 miles).

The first views of the east side appear at Bear Gap. Turn left and hike north on the PCT as it climbs and enters Pickhandle Basin. This is a great section

© SCOTT LEONARD

scenic views on the way to Bear Gap

of trail, as it passes through a large avalanche chute above Pickhandle Basin. The PCT reaches a second signed junction at Pickhandle Gap (4.1 miles). The PCT traverses the east side of Crown Point and reaches the best stretch of this hike, where the view to the south is remarkable. Craggy American Ridge stands across the valley, while Goat Rocks and Mount Adams loom on the horizon. The hike reaches another signed junction (4.5 miles), where the route turns left to remain on the PCT.

Although the hike only gains 1,800 feet, much of the first five miles is a steady climb. The final ascent occurs as the PCT climbs to Blue Bell Pass (5.0 miles). This is the high point of the hike, at 6,300 feet, offering a good view across the valley to the barren ski slopes. Just beyond Blue Bell Pass, Bullion Basin Trail reaches yet another junction (5.1 miles). Turn left on Bullion Basin Trail, as it drops into the basin and encounters a large horse camp. This steep section is a constant descent and hard on the knees. The trail then reaches the access road (7.3 miles), the final segment leading down to the trailhead.

Directions

From Seattle, drive east on I-90 to I-405. Turn south and drive to Exit 4/Highway 169. Drive south 25 miles to Enumclaw. Follow signs to Highway 410 and turn east, toward Mount Rainier. Drive 32 miles to Crystal Mountain Boulevard/Forest Service Road 7166. Turn left and drive six miles toward Crystal Mountain Ski Resort. Turn left on a small gravel road just after Parking Lot C but before East Peak Center. The gravel road reaches a T in 50 yards. The signed trailhead is 25 yards to the right of the T intersection.

Information and Contact

This trail is accessible June–September and is open to hikers, leashed dogs, and horses. A federal Northwest Forest Pass is required to park here. For a map of Mount Baker–Snoqualmie National Forest, contact the Outdoor Recreation Information Center at the downtown Seattle REI. For topographic maps, ask Green Trails for No. 239, Lester, or ask the USGS for Norse Peak. For more information, contact Mount Baker–Snoqualmie National Forest, Enumclaw Ranger Station, 450 Roosevelt Avenue East, Enumclaw, WA 98022, 360/825-6585.

RESOURCES

© SCOTT LEONARD

MAP SYMBOLS

- - - - - ·	Featured Trail	(80)	Interstate Freeway	○	City/Town
- - - - - ·	Other Trail	(101)	US Highway	✗ ✗	Airfield/Airport
═══════	Expressway	(29)	State Highway	⌇	Golf Course
═══════	Primary Road	66	County Highway	🝮	Waterfall
───────	Secondary Road	❚	Trailhead	▦	Swamp
- - - - - - - - -	Unpaved Road	★	Point of Interest	▲	Mountain
················	Ferry	ⓟ	Parking Area	♠	Park
— · — · — ·	National Border	⋀	Campground	\\	Pass
— ·· —	State Border	▪	Other Location	✦	Unique Natural Feature

Resources

NATIONAL PARKS
Mount Rainier National Park
Wilkeson Wilderness Information Center
P.O. Box 423
Wilkeson, WA 98396
360/569-6020

NATIONAL FORESTS
Mount Baker-Snoqualmie National Forest
www.fs.fed.us/r6/mbs

Verlot Public Service Center
33515 Mountain Loop Highway
Granite Falls, WA 98252
360/691-7791

Darrington Ranger District
1405 Emmens Street
Darrington, WA 98241
360/436-1155

Skykomish Ranger District
74920 Northeast Stevens
  Pass Highway
P.O. Box 305
Skykomish, WA 98288
360/677-2414

Snoqualmie Ranger District, Enumclaw Ranger Station
450 Roosevelt Avenue East
Enumclaw, WA 98022
360/825-6585

Snoqualmie Ranger District, North Bend Ranger Station
42404 Southeast North Bend Way
North Bend, WA 98045
425/888-1421

Olympic National Forest
www.fs.fed.us/r6/olympic

Quilcene Ranger District
295142 U.S. 101 South
P.O. Box 280
Quilcene, WA 98376
360/765-2200

Wenatchee National Forest
www.fs.fed.us/r6/wenatchee

Cle Elum Ranger District
803 West 2nd Street
Cle Elum, WA 98922
509/852-1100

PARKS, RECREATION AREAS, AND OTHER RESOURCES
Seattle City Parks and Recreation
100 Dexter Avenue North
Seattle, WA 98109
206/684-4075
www.cityofseattle.net/parks

Washington Department of Natural Resources
P.O. Box 47001
Olympia, WA 98504-7001
360/902-1375

**Washington State Parks and
Recreation Commission**
P.O. Box 42650
Olympia, WA 98504-2669
360/902-8844 (information) or
360/902-8500 (State Parks Pass)
www.parks.wa.gov

MAP RESOURCES
Green Trails
P.O. Box 77734
Seattle, WA 98177
206/546-MAPS (206/546-6277)
www.greentrails.com

**Outdoor Recreation
Information Center**
in the Seattle REI building
222 Yale Avenue North
Seattle, WA 98109-5429
206/470-4060

USGS Information Services
Box 25286
Denver, CO 80225
www.usgs.gov
888/275-8747

HIKING CLUBS
AND GROUPS
Cascade Chapter of the Sierra Club
180 Nickerson Street
Suite 202
Seattle, WA 98109-1631
206/523-2147
www.cascade.sierraclub.org

Mountaineers
300 3rd Avenue West
Seattle, WA 98119
206/284-8484
www.mountaineers.org

Mountains-to-Sound Greenway
1011 Western Avenue
Suite 606
Seattle, WA 98104
206/812-0122
www.mtsgreenway.org

Pacific Northwest Trail Association
P.O. Box 1817
Mount Vernon, WA 98273
877/854-9415
www.pnt.org

Washington Trails Association
1305 4th Avenue
Suite 512
Seattle, WA 98101-2401
206/625-1367
www.wta.org

HIKING WEBSITES
Attrition Hiking Guide
www.attrition.ws

Washington Hikes
www.washingtonhikes.com

Index

Acknowledgments

Writing a hiking guide is never easy, not even if it's the second go-around. I would like to thank friends who shared in adventures on the trail: Louise Alexander, Erica Capuana, Ben Cate, and Dave Dow. To all who helped contribute information for my first book, *Foghorn Outdoors Washington Hiking*, thank you—your support again proved indispensable. And a big thank you goes to Patti Bleifuss and Chris Duval, who contributed numerous photos for this guide—you helped save my hide! And thanks to Green Trails Maps, whose donation of maps was invaluable.

To write a hiking guide that covers my favorite parts of Washington fulfilled a long-time dream. Thanks to parents, teachers, mentors, and friends who have taught and inspired me throughout my life—this book is as much yours as mine.